Hope Does Not Disappoint
Choosing Joy Amidst Suffering

Christine Yager

ISBN: 9798668330485

All Scripture quotations, unless otherwise indicated,
are taken from the New American Standard Bible, ®
copyright © 1960, 1962, 1963, 1968, 1971, 1972,
1973, 1975, 1977, 1995 by The Lockman
Foundation. Used by permission.

All Greek dictionary definitions were taken from
Thayer and Smith, The NAS New Testament Greek
Lexicon, 1999.

www.christineyager.com

DEDICATION

To my husband, Michael, for choosing to love me as we walk through this life together. Your love and support means so much to me. To my daughters, Elizabeth, Katherine, and Eleanor – I pray you know how much you are loved by Dad and me, and most importantly, our Good and Gracious God. Each of you were prayed and hoped for and are such wonderful gifts to me. And to every woman who has felt the sting of infertility – you are so much more than what your body can or cannot do. I pray you know how much our God delights in you.

CONTENTS

FORWARD

No one likes pain. In fact, we do everything in our power to avoid going there. So why do we, as believers in Christ, think that our lives will be peaceful and free of trials?

Jesus said in John 16:33, "I have told you all this so that you may have peace in me. Here on earth you will have many trials and sorrows. But take heart, because I have overcome the world." Even though we have been lovingly warned by Christ to expect trials, we are oftentimes surprised when things go wrong.

Because we live in a fallen world, trials of various shapes and sizes will come our way. There are three responses we can choose when faced with disappointments: We can get mad at God and rail at Him for not taking care of us in the way we desire. We can harden our hearts by stuffing our pain and becoming flat and emotionless in our relationship with the Lord. Or we can press into the Holy One and find His comfort and peace in the midst of our grief.

Christine Yager intimately shares the struggles she experienced as a teen and young Christian and how she learned that God loves her and desires an intimate relationship with her. But when faced with a devastating miscarriage and the loss of the dream of becoming a mother in her desired timing, she candidly admits that she wrestled with Him. In time, however, when her strength and energy ran out and she was at the end of herself, she found that she was in a good place. For this is where she surrendered her will to the Holy One and chose to press into all that she knew to be true about Him. And in this act of relinquishment, she experienced divine transformation that changed her whole outlook on life.

As she walked out her faith even though her circumstances were hard, Christine learned that the Lord is always present, no matter what we're facing. He has conquered fear and is ever ready to help us walk through every trial and disappointment life brings. She found that His presence may not always prevent us from falling, but He is always standing guard to help us get back up...if we choose to trust Him. And if our hearts are tender, when we are in the depths of sorrow, we will be able to recognize more fully how much God loves and cares for us.

We live in a fallen world where every person will experience suffering in some form or another. Overcoming the devastation caused by heartbreaking disappointment is not an easy task. Thankfully, Christine has gifted us with a book of hope. Every sentence is a reflection of what it means to truly trust God in the midst of the brokenness of life. Recognizing that suffering is inevitable, Christine chose to allow her pain to bring glory to the Lord by sharing her story. And as you walk with her through the pages of this book, you will connect with her pain and find comfort and hope in her faith and hope in God. Like Christine, by pressing into the Holy One and holding tightly to His hands, you will see that truly, hope does not disappoint.

Bev DeSalvo
Author, Return to Joy

ACKNOWLEDGMENTS

A special thanks to my husband, Michael, for encouraging me from beginning to end. Thank you for loving me even when I am not lovable. You have taught me so much and demonstrated Christ's love for His Bride. I'm so thankful to be your bride, and I wouldn't want to live this life with any other partner.

Also a special thanks to April Erwin for editing my book and providing advice along the way. You should check out her books at www.aprilerwin.com.

Another special thanks to Bev DeSalvo for writing the forward for my book and encouraging me along the way.

And last but not least, I want to thank my family and friends who have supported, prayed for, and encouraged me throughout every trial I share in this book. Your love and friendship helped me to not feel alone.

PROLOGUE

I had it all planned out. I would buy some baby shoes and present them to my husband along with the joyous news that I'm pregnant. Then a few days later, on Christmas morning, we'd share the news with our families. There would be gasps of excitement, lots of hugs, and maybe some tears as the future grandparents began to accept the reality that their babies would soon have a baby of their own.

But then five days before Christmas, I was surprised to have to get the box of feminine products from the cabinet. Definitely not pregnant. A little disappointed that it didn't happen on the first try, I adjusted my plan. Instead of telling our families on Christmas morning, we would buy them a coffee mug or some knick-knack that says "World's Greatest Grandparent" and just give it to them on whichever day we decided to share our news. Again, I imagined lots of hugs and excitement. But another month proved unsuccessful.

And I do mean unsuccessful, as my mind began to switch into what I call Control Mode. It's the frame of mind that only sees my circumstances as victories or losses. It's how I get when I know there is a lot to learn about a subject, and if I just put in the time and effort, anything can be accomplished.

So to the Internet I went, researching all the ways to determine when you ovulate, how to track your cycles, and how to give you your best chances at conceiving. You wouldn't believe all the acronyms commonly used! I also read several books on the subject, downloaded an app to assist with my tracking, and started an Excel file to document all the data I was collecting (putting that engineering education to good use).

It became an obstacle for me to overcome. And upon achieving my victory over this, I could be that much more excited about what I had accomplished. Through these first few months, I began to see my poor husband as simply the necessary ingredient to help create a baby.

Needless to say, I had a very unhealthy mindset, but I didn't know it at the time. I was also causing resentment and strain in our marriage. I had the completely ridiculous idea that somehow I had control over the ability to create life, or that at the very least, God needed my help with that job. As the months turned into years of waiting, I really struggled with my view of God.

Many months before we began trying to get pregnant, I was a week late for my period. Having never been all that excited about having children in my early twenties, I remember feeling surprised at my disappointment when the pregnancy test came back negative. In the months that followed, that disappointment took root as a desire to be a mom – a desire I believe came from the Lord. He had changed my heart and gave me that desire. I waited many months for my husband to feel comfortable with the decision to try to conceive, praying that he would trust the Lord with our future and timing. I was delighted when my husband finally agreed that it was okay for us to start trying. At the time, I thought that was all there was to it – just a decision couples make, and then pregnancy would surely follow. After all, wasn't that the message in sex-ed classes growing up? Thou shalt use protection lest you *will* get pregnant...like it's a certainty, a cause-and-effect relationship.

So given my naiveté and Control Mode mindset, I wrestled a lot with the idea that God had given me this desire to be a mom and then had the audacity to not fulfill that desire when I wanted. It felt...personal. I began to question what I had done to deserve this punishment, more evidence of my skewed perspective of God. I began to question my right to call myself a woman. After all, my body couldn't even do what a woman's body was created to do. I blamed myself, my mistakes, my husband, his mistakes, and God for forgetting me in my pain. I felt overlooked and left behind as I saw friend after friend announce their pregnancies, and have one or more child...all while I was still waiting.

But God knew something I didn't know. He knows *everything*. He knew the beginning and the end of our story, long before we started living it. And as you will hopefully see as you continue to read this book, God taught me so much about Himself through my story. Through my pain and suffering, I learned what it means to trust God – really *trust* Him. Even before we became parents, I reached a place in my journey where I was truly thankful for our infertility because of the growth that had taken place in our hearts, marriage, and lives. We are forever changed and forever grateful, and I wouldn't change a thing that has happened because it all led to who and where we are today, as well as who we are still becoming.

My hope for you reading this book is that you might relate to how it feels to experience suffering and to recognize that God is always and only good. My hope is that you will understand and truly believe that God loves you. Not because He has to or because He made you, but because He wants to. I want you to believe that He made you *because* He loves you, not the other way around. If you can come to accept these truths, then I hope to show you that you can experience suffering but still choose joy. I hope to show you that choosing to hope in the Lord is never futile because hope does not disappoint.

CHAPTER 1

Suffering is Inevitable

I have loved horses for as long as I can remember. My mom tells me that my love for horses began after I saw the movie *The Black Stallion* at two or three years old. She got me a plastic toy black stallion horse, and I remember trying to ride it around the living room (I don't think this toy lasted very long before its legs broke off from trying to carry a little girl that far exceeded its weight load limit). When I was four years old, my parents graciously began paying for me to take horseback riding lessons. For those of you who are familiar with horseback riding, you are probably chuckling at the mental image of a toddler trying to ride a normal sized horse – my legs didn't come close to resting on his sides where they are supposed to. This beautiful, forgiving creature patiently walked around the arena while my little legs kicked and kicked his upper rib cage.

My love for horses continued to grow over the years. At five years old, I began begging my parents to buy me a horse of my own. When they said no, I remember being determined to save up all my allowance money to buy my own horse one day. But having enough money to purchase a horse was only one hurdle I had to figure out how to jump. I also had to figure out where to keep a horse because we did not live in the country. I remember calling the phone number on a for sale sign for a piece of commercial property within walking distance of our house to see how much they were asking for their land. There's a gas station and a fast food restaurant there now, so I'm guessing that the owners of those businesses gave them a better offer than what my weekly allowance rate of a couple dollars per week could offer.

In the meantime, I kept taking horseback riding lessons and loved learning about horses. The young woman who taught my horse lessons was so sweet and encouraging. I soon had a favorite lesson horse named Chance, and when I was about ten years old, my riding instructor encouraged me to enter the local schooling show. I remember being sick with a cold that weekend but wanted to compete anyway. I was pleasantly surprised when we won second place in both classes!

During a lesson a few weeks later, my beloved Chance started misbehaving. While cantering around the ring, he took off running and refused to stop no matter how hard I tried to pull the reins to stop him. Around and around the ring we went, my energy and strength quickly draining as I exhausted myself pulling the reins and trying not to fall off. The instructor kept trying to approach him, but as soon as she would get close, he bolted the other direction, beginning the terrifying spree time and time again. Eventually, my strength and balance gave out, and I tumbled to the ground. It was the first time I had ever fallen off a horse. I was relieved the frightening ordeal was over but was still trembling with fear as the adrenaline continued to course through my body.

But my instructor did something critical that I will never forget – after hopping on Chance to get him under control, she hopped off and immediately walked him back to me and made me get back on. *You've got to be kidding me! Did you see what this horse just did to me?!* But in hindsight, I am *so* grateful for her actions. Had she not forced me to immediately get back on, I likely would have allowed the fear of that experience to keep me from riding again.

With the law of gravity, falling is inevitable. Everyone falls sometimes. What matters is how you get back up again.

My riding instructor guided me through that frightening experience. She was present while Chance was running off with me, and she was present afterwards.

Just like God. Always present, no matter what you're facing. Ready to help you face your fears because He already conquered fear. His presence won't stop you from falling sometimes, but He is ready to help you get back up if you choose to trust Him. Sometimes you have to fall in order to recognize how loved and cared for you are. Just like my strength and energy eventually ran out, there's a similar surrender in reaching the end of yourself and choosing to trust God instead.

❦

I always struggled with self-confidence. In preschool, I was teased because my arms were "too hairy." In elementary school, I had to wear glasses, and my lack of fashion sense didn't help when I picked out large, pink, coke-bottle frames. Then came braces for my teeth, head gear and all. Picture Darla from *Finding Nemo*, and then add big glasses. In middle school, I finally got contact lenses and the braces came off, making my physical appearance much more attractive. But when you struggle with self-confidence, you can't convince even a supermodel that they're pretty. I grew up always seeing myself as an ordinary, nothing special type of girl – the type of girl who never turns a guy's head.

This view of myself developed for a variety of different reasons, but the root of it was a lack of understanding that my worth comes from the Lord instead of the world. Due to this misunderstanding of self-worth, I entered high school and college with the mindset that I'm only as valuable as a guy says I am.

In high school, the guys were not interested in dating me because I was pretty publicly dedicated to not having sex before marriage. So, even though I had crushes on lots of guys, I never had a boyfriend and attended all of the school dances with my girl friends. This really fed into my self-confidence struggles because I felt like no one was willing to accept me. Then in college, being one of the few females majoring in engineering, I suddenly had no trouble getting a date. But I was heartbroken each and every time I liked a guy who it inevitably didn't work out with (again because I wasn't willing to have sex before marriage). I just wanted someone to love me for being me, not for what my body could give them.

Even though I became a Christian back in high school, I never felt accepted by my peers in the church I attended, so in college I eventually stopped attending. This meant that I had no support system in place to encourage me with my dating woes. I worked as a waitress at a local billiards bar, so I certainly wasn't meeting guys at church. I compromised my morals a little bit, thinking maybe if I was willing to do just a little more physically with a guy, then he would finally accept me. Alas, it made no difference and only resulted in more hurt feelings when the relationship ended. No wonder I was in that lose-lose predicament.

After getting hurt and dumped too many times, I began to struggle with depression and hopelessness. Everywhere I went it seemed there were happy couples in my field-of-view, constantly reminding me of what I didn't have. I started to doubt that there was even a *decent* guy out there, let alone *the* guy God wanted me to marry. Would I have to settle for someone or something less than what I had dreamed of?

◦──◦❦◦──◦

There are countless ways that mankind experiences suffering. It's everywhere: in the news, social media, movies/TV, music, your friends, your family, and likely in your own life. Suffering is a worldwide epidemic that has no cure and no immunity. Because we live in a fallen world – a world with sin – all people will experience suffering in some form or another.

"Beloved, do not be surprised at the fiery ordeal among you, which comes upon you for your testing, as though some strange thing were happening to you."
1 Peter 4:12

Suffering was born the moment Adam and Eve took a bite of the fruit of the tree of the knowledge of good and evil, and suffering has permeated the lives of every human being that has been born since. The type, frequency, and depth of suffering may be as unique as each of us, but no one – absolutely no one – is immune to suffering.

A tempting question you have likely asked yourself at least once before is: How could God let bad things happen? If you internalize that question, you may ask: Is God punishing me? In the next chapter I'll discuss the purpose behind suffering, but for now let's focus on where suffering comes from. Who or what is behind the reality that we all suffer?

The short answer of why bad things happen is *sin*. We live in a broken, sin-filled world with broken bodies, where each person has the free will to make their own choices for better or worse. A person's individual choices may have tangible consequences on other people. And those consequences can result in more choices, and more consequences, and on and on like ripples spreading and colliding on the surface of water.

Furthermore, this world does not exist in the original state as God intended. He created perfect paradise, but mankind brought destruction by trusting in Satan and self more than the Creator. The world broke and remains broken to this day. Disease, natural disasters, violence, and all kinds of evil began to rule this world. Paramount to these was an evil one who wasn't satisfied with serving God. He wanted to *be* God.

"⁸Be of sober spirit, be on the alert. Your adversary, the devil, prowls around like a roaring lion, seeking someone to devour. ⁹But resist him, firm in your faith, knowing that the same experiences of suffering are being accomplished by your brethren who are in the world."
1 Peter 5:8-9

It's important to understand that God does not *cause* suffering. Suffering is the result of natural and supernatural consequences of sin. It says it clearly above – the devil is prowling and seeking to devour. Satan's subtle and overt tactics certainly lead to suffering. And sometimes suffering is just the natural consequence of sin being ever-present in this world.

God does not directly cause suffering, but He does *allow* it. Furthermore, if the suffering is a consequence of your or someone else's sin, then rest assured that Christ died for that. He felt the weight of that sin as He struggled for breath on the cross. He conquered it, and therefore can use your suffering and redeem it in unimaginable ways.

When you experience suffering, it doesn't mean that God is punishing you or that He doesn't love you. Suffering can be a part of God's plan for your life, either for character growth (discipline) or to point to Jesus. Remember, it was God's plan for Jesus to experience suffering, and God loves Jesus immensely! God didn't drive the nails into Jesus' flesh, but He allowed Jesus to experience this suffering for a very specific purpose...a purpose that ultimately brings Him glory and invites us into a relationship with Him.

Likewise, God loves you and has a plan to use your suffering for His glory, somehow, someway. You are not alone in your suffering. He is always present with you, even during your suffering. He is present before, during, and after your fall to the ground.

Though your specific suffering may be unique, you are not unlucky or the only person who suffers – the whole world suffers too. A pastor at my church once said that you're either just coming out of suffering, in the middle of it, or about to suffer. It's not "if," but "when." No one can escape it because we are all human beings living in a world that contains and breeds suffering.

No amount of money, good deeds, prayer, or faith will prevent suffering from coming upon you from time to time. God does not promise to protect you from experiencing suffering, but He does promise to never leave your side when that suffering comes. Jesus Himself suffered, arguably the most of all.

"²¹For you have been called for this purpose, since Christ also suffered for you, leaving you an example for you to follow in His steps, ²²who committed no sin, nor was any deceit found in His mouth; ²³and while being reviled, He did not revile in return; while suffering, He uttered no threats, but kept entrusting Himself to Him who judges righteously; ²⁴and He Himself bore our sins in His body on the cross, so that we might die to sin and live to righteousness; for by His wounds you were healed."
1 Peter 2:21-24

Notice that experiencing suffering has nothing to do with your behavior or whether you deserve to suffer or not. If anyone had a right to brag about their good behavior, it was Jesus. He "committed no sin, nor was any deceit found in His mouth," yet He experienced suffering. Clearly He didn't deserve to suffer, but He did suffer – not because of His actions, but because He chose to subject Himself to this broken world full of its temptations and hardships. But because He was perfect and sinless, we have His example to follow of how to respond to suffering: He "kept entrusting Himself" to God the Father. This is a key aspect to suffering well that took me many years to recognize as the way to respond to suffering.

When I was 20 years old, while working one night during the winter break of my sophomore year, a witty and outgoing 18-year-old guy weaseled his way into my life. That's right...I met my husband in a bar. God can work anywhere, right?

Still struggling with depression, I was immediately drawn to Michael like a breath of fresh air. He had such a positive outlook on life, especially for someone who had already been through the wringer at such a young age. His father died of cancer when he was nine, leaving his mother and him to struggle month-to-month. They moved around a lot too, so Michael didn't have a stable childhood. Then, while he was in high school, his mother was diagnosed with breast cancer (for the first time).

All of this contributed to him having a bit of a wild streak in his high school years. He became a Christian at the end of his senior year of high school and barely had a high enough GPA to graduate (not because he isn't smart, but because he viewed high school as a waste of time). When I was in high school, getting good grades was my sport, my whole mission – I graduated fourth in my class of nearly 600. I like to joke that it's a good thing we didn't meet during high school because we probably would not have liked one another. After he graduated, he wanted to attend the local community college but took the fall semester off to work to save up money for tuition. It was during the winter break between semesters that we met.

He later told me that a few days before we met, he had prayed to God, asking Him to bring a Christian girl into his life. He desired to have a serious girlfriend, tired of having casual encounters like he did in high school. On the night we met, he didn't want to go out because he had to wake up early for work the next morning, but his friends convinced him to go play pool with them...at the billiards bar that I was working at that night. God is in the details. Every detail.

Michael and his friends were playing pool in my section, but since they were all minors, I didn't spend that much time at their table because I knew they couldn't order anything except soft drinks. Michael jokes that it was like I had a motor on my butt...I just sped on by, which left him scrambling for an excuse to get to talk to me. So on my next time around, he stopped me and asked me what time it was (even though he had a cell phone in his pocket and a watch on his wrist). After telling him the time, I continued making the rounds.

Realizing that he needed another way to get my attention, he asked his friend to strike up a conversation with one of my waitress friends. When I stopped to also talk to my friend,

Michael seized the opportunity to talk to me. Smooth operator!

At the time, I was casually dating a guy that I wasn't really interested in because he wanted things to get more serious, but this guy was there that night waiting for me to get off work. I called him the "creepy stalker guy" to my waitress friend and was complaining to her about how I didn't want to date him anymore, and I just wished he would get the hint already. Michael jumped into the conversation and asked me, "Have you told him how you feel?" I said, "Well, kinda, sorta." And Michael said, "Well, that's kinda sorta why he's still here." I laughed and started to enjoy talking to him more.

We had really hit it off that night. So when the night was coming to an end, I said in a flirty way to Michael, "You know, it would probably make the creepy stalker guy jealous if I gave you my phone number right now." He simply replied with, "You're right, it probably would." And then he turned around and walked away as he left with his friends. A little perplexed at why he didn't take my offer of getting my number, I brushed it off and went about my night. But thankfully, Michael had asked me earlier that night when I would be working again.

So a couple of days later while I was working, Michael approached me and officially asked me out on a date. I snarkily replied, "Sure, but you'll probably need my number for that!" He humbly said, "Yeah...can I have it?"

That was on a Saturday, and he told me that he would call me on Tuesday to go out that night. But the thing I appreciated about him was that he couldn't wait and called me on Monday instead. When he called that night to discuss our first date, he had three options in mind. He first asked, "Do you want to go out for dinner tonight?" It was already early in the evening, so I answered, truthfully, "I already ate." On to Plan B he asked, "Ok, would you like to go see *Meet the Fockers* in the theater tonight?" Again, truthfully, "Well, I already saw it in the theater." Last option, third time's the charm! He asked, "We could rent a movie instead?" As a big fan of movies, I again answered truthfully, "I'm sorry, I already rented four movies." For some reason, he started to think I was shooting him down completely (I can't imagine why, ha!). So I suggested instead that we go play pool. And that was our first date – playing pool and staying up most of that night talking to get to know one another.

We fell in love pretty quickly. Both being the type of people who openly share their hearts, we quickly learned about one another's lives and past baggage. The key difference in this new relationship from all the previous ones I had had was that we both believed in Jesus Christ and wanted to honor Him. Within two months of dating, we had already discussed that marriage was in our future and what we wanted to name our future children.

We met weekly with an older married couple for discipleship. This couple, David and Sue, helped lay a healthy foundation in our relationship. David had been the one who first shared the gospel with Michael at the end of his senior year of high school. As another example of how God is in every detail, I want to share more about this story.

David, Sue, and their four children had moved to our city to work at a church that ended up not being able to hire them after all. It was the only reason they had moved to our city – to work at that church – so it would be a while before they made plans to move elsewhere. And since they were fully funded by ministry donations, David and Sue decided to try to make the best of a bad situation and go to work on their own while living in this city – they literally went around knocking on people's doors in the hopes of being able to share the gospel with others. They typically did this in apartment complexes because of the close proximity, large college student population, and many international students in the city who have likely never heard about Christ.

One afternoon they knocked on Michael's door. David and Sue would begin each conversation by asking if they could ask some spiritual awareness survey questions (inspired by the Kennedy questions). The answers to the questions would quickly reveal if the participant believed in Christ or not. The first question asked, "On a scale of 1 to 10 (with 10 being the most sure), how sure are you that if you die tonight that you would spend eternity in heaven?" Michael answered "7," figuring that he was a decently good person. The second question David asked was, "If you die tonight and stand before God at the gates of heaven and He asks you why He should let you in, what would you say?" Michael said he had no idea what he'd say. David asked if he could share a quick pamphlet with him that would help him with these answers, but Michael said no because he was about to eat lunch (he's always been a big eater). But David asked if he could come back about an hour later, and Michael agreed.

So later that afternoon David returned and shared the gospel with Michael. Having never heard the gospel presented that clearly before, Michael was surprised to learn that salvation is a free gift of grace offered by God, and trusting in Christ and Christ alone (not your own efforts in any way) is all that one needs to do in order to become a Christian. Making that decision grants you eternal entrance into heaven and nothing can ever change that. So Michael chose to trust in Christ in that moment and then understood that he could now answer with "10" and "Because I trusted in Christ," fully bringing to life Ephesians 2:8-9.

But being a Christian doesn't preclude you from experiencing suffering.

❦

After several months of dating and being discipled by David and Sue, Michael admitted to me that he struggled with viewing pornography and wanted to stop, so he asked me to ask him about it every couple of weeks. Still naïve to this struggle, I obliged and asked him every so often how he was doing in that area. His answer for about six months was "Fine" or "Good." I had no reason to distrust his answers, so I remember thinking, "Wow, how amazing that he so easily overcame that struggle!" and checked it off my mental list of criteria I desired my future husband to have.

In December of the same year – almost a year into our dating relationship – we were shopping at the mall and just kept bickering over insignificant things. Angry and tired of fighting, I responded in my usual way back then – gave up and withdrew by walking back to the car to wait for him to eventually come back.

When he joined me in the car, we sat there in silence for a while. But then he said something that made my heart drop: "Christine, I've been lying to you for the past six months. When you asked me about how I was doing in my struggle with pornography, I lied. I've still been viewing it often and it's a big problem."

I was devastated. How could he lie to me for so long? The past six months now felt completely fake. Was I not pretty enough, so he had to satisfy his eyes elsewhere? Was he secretly not okay with us waiting to have sex until we were married, just like all the past guys I had dated or been rejected by? How could I possibly compete with the perfect looking supermodels in porn even once we were married and having sex? My mind was flooded with so many painful thoughts and fears.

After a big fight about this, I remember yelling at him basically giving him an ultimatum: it's either me or *those* women. He reassured me that he desperately wanted to stop.

The months that followed were some of my darkest moments. Enter my Control Mode – the mindset I get when I think I know best about how to handle life – the very opposite of entrusting myself to God as Christ's example shows. As I jumped into Control Mode, insisting that Michael share every lustful thought with me in the name of total honesty, my heart slowly started cracking. And the cracks did what they do best: grew bigger.

My trust with Michael was so broken and would take many years to heal. I felt so paranoid and fearful about getting hurt or lied to again that I became completely obsessive about this whole thing.

I remember countless times that I scrutinized his Internet

history, equally terrified of getting hurt yet desperate to never be lied to and made a fool of again. There were many times that I found illicit browser history and questioned him about it. He would often deny it, fearing my judgment. His denial fueled my fear, anger, and distrust, which fueled my Control Mode mindset to dig deeper in order to help repair the betrayal he caused. My judgment and lack of forgiveness fueled his shame, bitterness, and desire to keep his sin hidden from me. It also perpetuated his struggle with pornography because when you're trying desperately to not think about something (a pink elephant, for example), it's of course the only thing you're going to think about! Psychology calls this ironic process theory.

He tried some accountability groups, but he felt they were no help because they were filled with peers only, and no one opened up vulnerably about their struggles. His lack of accountability also fueled my Control Mode. Grappling for more and more control over him merely led to him feeling more and more judged by me. That in turn led to bitterness that grew in both of our hearts. This will always be the result of a life without grace.

Now I want to interject here and reemphasize how wrong I was to treat him this way. Feeling hurt by his betrayal was to be expected and was a natural consequence of his sin. But judging, controlling, and not forgiving him were all wrong and very damaging to our relationship. Especially when I tell you what I'm about to tell you. You see, pornography is not a habit that only men struggle with. And pornography is not something that only Michael had struggled with. I too had a history with porn.

❦

In the present Internet-age, it's more and more common for women to struggle with viewing porn too. And while women's brains may be wired differently than men's brains to not be as visually stimulated, it by no means suggests that women cannot become addicted to viewing porn. The impact on the human brain when viewing porn is virtually the same as what happens when a human uses drugs – it's an intense and appealing dopamine hit that, with consistent use, can create neural pathways in the brain that have physical cravings to repeat. Desensitization can occur where longer and longer sessions and more and more intense, violent, or fetish-like porn is required to produce the same dopamine hit.

A person's reasons for viewing porn may be totally unrelated to sexual desire, such as feeling sad or worthless. Sometimes people develop a bad habit as a way of coping with pain, and for many, porn is one of those bad habits. I encourage you to learn more about the negative impacts of viewing porn if you are interested. Even if you personally haven't struggled with it, it's a guarantee you know someone who has, and it can be helpful to understand the science behind what's happening. FightTheNewDrug.org is a great resource to start with.

When I was a young child, there was no Internet. Porn had to be purchased, either on television or in physical format (VHS tapes, magazines, etc.) I was six years old when I was first exposed to porn. I was spending the night at my friend's house, and her dad had Playboy magazines in his bedroom that we looked at. I don't remember the specific details of each image this many years later, but I remember feeling like what I was seeing was wrong. But it also made me feel curious.

Shortly after that, on a different night I slept over at this friend's house, we watched one of the sexually explicit movies on Cinemax (or "Skinemax" as it's often called). We knew we were not supposed to watch these movies. We quickly changed the channel if we even thought we heard her parents approaching the room. But we kept watching these types of movies with the excuse that we were gaining experience for our future husbands. (The enemy can think of almost any excuse imaginable to justify sin, can't he?)

I knew what I was doing was wrong. I felt guilty. But I didn't stop this destructive behavior. Five years later, I had made plans to spend the night at her house one night. But before I fell asleep there, I just felt so overcome with guilt for having watched yet another movie that I decided I was going to walk home (it wasn't that far). It was on that walk home in the middle of the night that I realized I was a sinner and I desperately needed a Savior. Even though I had grown up going to church and believing Jesus was real, I hadn't believed yet that *I* needed saving.

But that night was different. I knew that because I had sinned, I deserved to go to hell, and that terrified me. So I chose to believe in Jesus in that moment. But my understanding of the free gift of grace was lacking, so in my mind, I believed that I was only forgiven up to the most recent moment that I asked for God to forgive me. For example, if I sinned all week, then prayed Friday night asking God to forgive me and I died that night, then I was covered and would be accepted into heaven. But if I sinned on Saturday and then died before getting a chance to pray again, then I would be sent to hell. It may sound silly, but this was what I believed. Because of that, I lived in a constant state of fear and doubting whether I was truly saved or not. And I sin so often that even my fear of hell didn't stop me from sinning time and time again, including viewing porn.

Over the next several years, instead of just watching these porn movies while I was at my friend's house, I got clever and realized that I could record them on VHS and then watch them at my house too! I used to check the TV guide schedule and plan which nights to spend the night at this friend's house in order to be able to record new movies.

After I watched a movie, I would feel overcome with guilt and shame. I believed I had let God down again. But my habit of watching these movies continued, despite my fears, shame, and guilt.

When the Internet became commonly available in middle school and we had a computer in our house, I viewed porn there too. Some friends at school also had more hardcore porn movies that I borrowed, though that content was beginning to exceed what I felt comfortable watching.

During this time, I felt stuck in a vicious cycle. I hated what I was doing. I knew it was wrong. I wanted to stop but just couldn't stop. I also loved God and wanted to know Him more.

At the end of ninth grade, I was reading *Left Behind* by Tim LaHaye and Jerry Jenkins. They wrote a fictional book series about the end times in the 90s. While reading the first book – when one of the main characters finally understood that Jesus had died for his sins and that God's gift of salvation is freely offered to those who choose to accept it – it finally clicked with me that I have no reason to fear going to hell. If I admit that I'm a sinner, believe that Christ died for my sin, and trust that there's nothing I can possibly do on my own to be good enough to make up for my sin – it's only Christ that I'm relying on for my salvation – then I can *know* that when I die, I will go to heaven. No more fear and having to keep a clean slate of asking for forgiveness in case I die unexpectedly. No more doubting if God can forgive me for sinning, yet again. Jesus took care of that for me, once and for all. Every past and future sin was nailed to the cross. What freedom I felt in that moment! And such gratitude and humility. With my new, transformed heart I realized that I had no desire to keep the habit of viewing porn in my life. And so, after nine years of viewing porn, I stopped and didn't struggle with it again. But I was giving myself more credit with stopping than recognizing that God freed me from that struggle.

So, back to my relationship with Michael. It was very difficult at the time for me to have any empathy for him because, in my mind, I couldn't understand why Michael didn't just decide to stop viewing porn like I had. It seemed so simple: if you don't want to view it, just don't view it! So each time he chose to view porn and then told me (or I discovered it in the viewing history), I felt so angry and bitter because it felt like he was hurting me on purpose. Perhaps if I had understood the science behind a porn addiction, I might have been capable of responding with more understanding, but alas,

I couldn't have been further from understanding. I became more and more obsessed about catching him in a lie and demanding that he confess to me any time he "failed me." (I cringe at how legalistic and unkind I was, but I'm being transparent with you in the hope that this somehow points you to Christ.)

This obsession and bitterness got so bad in our dating relationship that I considered ending it. There was one morning where I prayed to God, and I began to think that maybe Michael and I were not meant to be together anymore. All of this pain was just not worth it, I reasoned. Following that train of thought, I wondered about the man God might want me to marry. If I stayed with Michael, I might miss out on meeting this Mr. Right...when suddenly God interrupted my thoughts with the words "Marry him." I paused, feeling shocked and confused. I began to doubt what I heard, thinking maybe that's just what I wanted to hear, and started my train of thought again. I thought what I heard was silly, and there's no way that God spoke to me...but again God interrupted my thoughts with "No, I'm telling you this is your future husband, and I want you to marry him." I was still skeptical if I was actually hearing God speak to me, or just hearing my own thoughts, but then I heard "Look at 1 Corinthians 2:11." (And I've never been that great at memorizing Scripture, so I had no idea what it said until I looked it up.)

"11For who among men knows the thoughts of a man except the spirit of the man which is in him? Even so the thoughts of God no one knows except the Spirit of God. 12Now we have received, not the spirit of the world, but the Spirit who is from God, so that we may know the things freely given to us by God, 13which things we also speak, not in words taught by human wisdom, but in those taught by the Spirit, combining spiritual thoughts with spiritual words."
1 Corinthians 2:11-13

I knew that as a believer in Christ I too have the Spirit of God in me; therefore, through the Spirit we can also know the thoughts of God that He chooses to reveal. I was stunned but believed that God had just spoken to me in my thoughts and told me to marry Michael. I then heard, "It won't be easy, but see Hebrews 4:16." Again, not being familiar with that verse, I looked it up.

"Therefore let us draw near with confidence to the throne of grace, so that we may receive mercy and find grace to help in time of need."
Hebrews 4:16

That was my first encounter with the truth that God really cares about the details of our lives. He really cares about *me*, in a unique way that's just between Him and me. That was my first encounter with seeing God the Father as God, my loving, caring Dad. But I still had not learned how to trust Him when I experienced suffering.

After we got married in May 2007, I expected Michael's struggles with pornography to end, now that we were having sex. But to my disappointment, I learned that nothing much had changed. After allowing myself to get to such a high level of stress in demanding to know every lustful thought he had, I finally reached my human limitation to withstand those assaults. I reached the end of my self-effort to hear day in and day out about his struggle because I was relying on my own strength to try to forgive and trust him. And I just could not do that on my own anymore.

Instead of realizing in that moment that God supplies all the strength, forgiveness, and trust we will ever need, Michael and I decided to stop talking about that subject. "Ignorance is bliss" was my new mindset.

For the next several years of our marriage, I knew that he probably still struggled with pornography but had no idea how often or to what extent. During those years, we still grew closer to one another, but there was always this elephant in the room that neither of us wanted to talk about. I was still very distrustful of him and hurt by his betrayal and lack of desire to get accountability, and he was still very bitter about feeling judged by me and my lack of forgiveness. There's only so much closeness and intimacy you can have with your spouse when you're sharing the room with a giant elephant.

CHAPTER 2
Good Grief...
How to Suffer Well

Several years ago, Michael and I were off work for Christmas break. It was a particularly cold and wet winter, which in Texas just means that it's rainy and cold. In my opinion, it's the perfect weather to light a fire, keep cozy under a blanket, and hang out inside all day reading or watching movies.

So I was surprised when Michael announced that he was going to spend the break digging up a large section of grass in our backyard to plant fruit trees. After asking if I wanted to help (*Um, no thanks*), he bundled up and went outside with a shovel. Now when I say "a large section of grass," I mean about one-third of the grassy square footage in our backyard. And we have a larger-than-average backyard in our neighborhood. The 8-foot-wide "L" shaped area of grass he wanted to remove spanned the entire width of our lot along the back fence line, as well as along the entire length of one of our side fence lines. (And this was just Phase I in his mind. Over the next few years, he expanded his orchard into the front yard and essentially made our entire landscape edible plants or trees.)

In order to accomplish his mission, he had to remove all the St. Augustine grass in the area he wanted to plant trees in. For those unfamiliar with this type of grass, it can be difficult to remove because it is comprised of runners – strands that root into the ground every couple inches and sprout grass blades along the way. You end up with a very robust, thick, and woven yard – great at enduring harsh Texas summers, but a pain to remove because it's so well-rooted and interwoven. He first attempted to remove the grass using a shovel. But after realizing how long that would take, he decided to rent a sod cutter machine from the local hardware store. This handy machinery rolled up longer stretches of the grass, removing more grass with less effort. But it's not a perfect process – the edges of your path usually still have small patches of grass that you have to painstakingly remove later. You can't leave any grass segment that's rooted, because it will just spread and eventually take over.

Due to the wet winter we were having that year, his working conditions were especially brutal (our backyard retains a lot of moisture, so it was really muddy, especially after the carpet of grass was removed) with freezing weather, high humidity, and hard labor.

Something you should know about my husband is that he is what we call a Visionary or a Dreamer. For the entire time I've known him, he has always had dreams of various sizes. He loves to speak in detail about his dreams, as if we're seriously drawing up plans to make them happen. As a typical type A person, I struggled earlier in our marriage with this. I'm very practical-minded, so whenever he would start talking in detail about a particular dream – like he was formulating plans on how to make it a reality – I would start to get nervous because I thought he was completely serious and ready to pull the trigger so-to-speak.

For example, one time he shared a dream about wanting to replace the ceiling in our master bathroom with starlight panels that you could dim. He showed me specific websites and products as he spoke and said things like, "We could get this one because of [insert some amazing feature of this product]," and then asked, "So what do you think?" And my practical-minded self noticed the price of the product in question, recalled our budget and savings situation at that moment, and said something like, "It's pretty, but we can't afford that right now." This hurt his feelings because he felt like I was shooting down his dreamy idea. Furthermore, it made him feel like I didn't trust him to make wise decisions, such as to thoroughly research something before purchasing (which he does and is wonderful at).

We had several fights that roughly followed this pattern: him sharing a dream, me responding with negativity/realism, him getting his feelings hurt and getting angry with me for squashing his dreams, me responding with confusion and defensiveness because I think he's living in a fantasy land. We finally communicated well enough for me to realize that he just wanted to feel free to voice his dreams and desired that I get excited about his ideas, not focus on the practicality of them in that moment or list off the reasons why it may not work. I eventually learned that when he shares a dream – even if he shows me very detailed plans about something – he just wants me to dream with him, not make a decision right then. He doesn't pursue every dream idea he comes up with. But he does want to fully flesh out an idea to help decide if it's worth pursuing or not, and he wants me to be a part of that process with him. That helps me relax in the moment and just be able to respect and encourage his creative mind.

So, when he decided to plant a fruit orchard in our backyard, I wasn't sure how serious he was. But when he started physically removing the grass, I knew he was serious because that meant he had thoroughly researched and planned out the details of what he wanted to buy and plant. He's not the type to act rashly.

I admit, when I realized his seriousness about planting a fruit orchard and saw him toiling in the cold, wet yard, I was a little concerned because, in my mind, that was not the time of year that I thought you should plant things. I mean, you typically see advertisements for planting a garden in the springtime, not the dead of winter, right? I figured he had done his research, but I admit I had my doubts about the success of this endeavor.

My doubts were further intensified when the trees he bought from a nursery arrived. They looked *dead*. Every single tree was thin, maybe six to eight feet tall, and had no leaves. Not a single one. He amended the soil with various things and then carefully untangled the roots of a particular tree and planted it in the special place he had reserved for that tree. He did this for each tree.

When he was all finished, he brought me outside to proudly show off his fruit orchard. I don't normally act phony, but in this instance, staring at a huge, muddy patch of yard with bare, dead-looking trees sticking up out of the ground...I totally played the phony card. With gritted teeth I said, "Honey...that looks...wow...you worked so hard...that looks...that's a lot of trees!"

But like all transformations, all it needed was careful and tender preparation, time, and for God's plans to unfold. Michael had carefully prepared the soil to provide optimum nutrients to each tree. He had carefully untangled the roots of each tree before planting them in their special spot. With time, sunlight, and water, the bare, dead-looking trees soon came to life when the weather started to warm in early spring. Trees that seemed completely useless, dead, and broken soon filled with blossoms of white, pink, and magenta. Bees actively visited each blossom for weeks. Then tiny, green leaves began to grow...and grow and grow. Each year, the trees grew in height, width, and productivity. (One year we had so many peaches that we were giving away bucketfuls!)

Isn't that a lovely thought of how God loves and cares for us, His beloved children? He all-knowingly prepares the soil, tenderly and lovingly untangles our mess of roots, and gently guides us to the special place He has planned in advance for us to be. And then He proudly rejoices in His work and waits with excited anticipation of the beauty that He knows is yet to come but is not yet visible to us. Nothing escapes His notice or care. Not one cell in your body is outside His concern and love.

It was a lot easier to see Michael's vision in hindsight than when I was staring at bare, dead-looking trees. Thank the Lord that He can see the end from the beginning, right? I'm *so* thankful that God doesn't look at us like bare, dead-looking people that are useless for His kingdom. We certainly may *feel* that way sometimes, but that is never how He sees you. He is always the careful, loving, attentive Gardener, waiting for you to blossom and transform into what He desires you to be, according to His plans.

❧

Suffering is inevitable, but it also serves a purpose – suffering is meant to bring glory to God. Because everyone in this world experiences suffering, chances are, you will share a similar type of suffering with believers and non-believers alike. I don't mean to undermine your pain here, but rather point out something that wasn't immediately obvious to me: you have a relatable and immediate way to connect with other people when you choose to share vulnerably about your suffering.

In other words, by sharing about your suffering and all that God has done for you through it (even if the suffering is still happening), you are getting a chance to share a testimony with non-believers and to uplift and encourage believers to trust Christ through their suffering. It all points back to God. There is good that can be found in your grief.

Whatever your type of suffering is, I dare you to share it vulnerably with other people. I encourage you to share what God has taught you through it. Be open and watch the beauty of what happens. Vulnerability breeds vulnerability. And vulnerability deepens every relationship on this earth.

Now, a fair warning here: when you choose to share vulnerably with others, you are taking a risk. You are risking that your story may be received with insensitivity or even disdain. I hope this won't happen (to you or to me!), but it is a possibility. We are sinful, we make poor choices, and we will hurt others whether we mean to or not. But we are also not meant to live behind walls built to protect ourselves. We are not meant to live alone on islands. God built us for community because He exists in the perfect community of the Trinity. We are made in His image with a need for others to share life with.

"23 Let us hold fast the confession of our hope without wavering, for He who promised is faithful; 24 and let us consider how to stimulate one another to love and good deeds, 25 not forsaking our own assembling together, as is the habit of some, but encouraging one another; and all the more as you see the day drawing near."
Hebrews 10:23-25

When you are courageous and choose to share vulnerably with others, I believe that more often than not it will break the ice and establish a deeper connection with people in a way that little else can. I believe that it will bring hearts closer together and help you feel less alone in this world. Is there any greater feeling on this earth than to share a part of yourself with another person and be accepted and understood by them? Isn't that a risk worth taking?

In addition to connecting with others, it's good to share your suffering for the sake of glorifying God.

"14 But even if you should suffer for the sake of righteousness, you are blessed. And do not fear their intimidation, and do not be troubled, 15 but sanctify Christ as Lord in your hearts, always being ready to make a defense to everyone who asks you to give an account for the hope that is in you, yet with gentleness and reverence"
1 Peter 3:14-15

The world is watching you. Since both believers and non-believers experience suffering, when a non-believer knows that you are a believer, they are watching how you respond to your suffering. If you respond with hope and joy, you never know the potential impact that may have. Observers that notice your joyful response to suffering will likely question what could possibly make you respond that way. What an opportunity to share about your hope in Jesus.

"but to the degree that you share the sufferings of Christ, keep on rejoicing, so that also at the revelation of His glory you may rejoice with exultation."
1 Peter 4:13

It's important to understand that suffering is inevitable and is meant to bring glory to God. But what does that look like in a practical way? How then do we handle ourselves when that suffering comes? Let's reflect once again on the example of Jesus and His suffering.

"21For you have been called for this purpose, since Christ also suffered for you, leaving you an example for you to follow in His steps, 22who committed no sin, nor was any deceit found in His mouth; 23and while being reviled, He did not revile in return; while suffering, He uttered no threats, but kept entrusting Himself to Him who judges righteously; 24and He Himself bore our sins in His body on the cross, so that we might die to sin and live to righteousness; for by His wounds you were healed."
1 Peter 2:21-24

I love this example of Christ's response to suffering and how He "kept entrusting Himself" to God the Father. As I said before, this is a key aspect to suffering well that took me many years to learn (and I'm still learning).

Another example of Jesus experiencing suffering is found in John 11.

"1Now a certain man was sick, Lazarus of Bethany, the village of Mary and her sister Martha. 2It was the Mary who anointed the Lord with ointment, and wiped His feet with her hair, whose brother Lazarus was sick. 3So the sisters sent word to Him, saying, 'Lord, behold, he whom You love is sick.' 4But when Jesus heard this, He said, 'This sickness is not to end in death, but for the glory of God, so that the Son of God may be glorified by it.' 5Now Jesus loved Martha and her sister and Lazarus. 6So when He heard that he was sick, He then stayed two days longer in the place where He was."
John 11:1-6

We know from this passage that Jesus loved Lazarus, but upon hearing that Lazarus was sick, He did something that most would find very strange: He remained for two more days in the place where He was. Instead of rushing off to help immediately, He remained where He was. But Jesus had a perfect understanding of the purpose of suffering when He said that "this sickness is not to end in death, but for the glory of God, so that the Son of God may be glorified by it." Such an incredible example of faith! But that isn't all to uncover from this passage...

"¹¹This He said, and after that He said to them, 'Our friend Lazarus has fallen asleep; but I go, so that I may awaken him out of sleep.' ¹²The disciples then said to Him, 'Lord, if he has fallen asleep, he will recover.' ¹³Now Jesus had spoken of his death, but they thought that He was speaking of literal sleep. ¹⁴So Jesus then said to them plainly, 'Lazarus is dead, ¹⁵and I am glad for your sakes that I was not there, so that you may believe; but let us go to him.' ¹⁶Therefore Thomas, who is called Didymus, said to his fellow disciples, 'Let us also go, so that we may die with Him.'

¹⁷So when Jesus came, He found that he had already been in the tomb four days. ¹⁸Now Bethany was near Jerusalem, about two miles off; ¹⁹and many of the Jews had come to Martha and Mary, to console them concerning their brother. ²⁰Martha therefore, when she heard that Jesus was coming, went to meet Him, but Mary stayed at the house. ²¹Martha then said to Jesus, 'Lord, if You had been here, my brother would not have died. ²²Even now I know that whatever You ask of God, God will give You.' ²³Jesus said to her, 'Your brother will rise again.' ²⁴Martha said to Him, 'I know that he will rise again in the resurrection on the last day.' ²⁵Jesus said to her, 'I am the resurrection and the life; he who believes in Me will live even if he dies, ²⁶and everyone who lives and believes in Me will never die. Do you believe this?' ²⁷She said to Him, 'Yes, Lord; I have believed that You are the Christ, the Son of God, even He who comes into the world.'

²⁸When she had said this, she went away and called Mary her sister, saying secretly, 'The Teacher is here and is calling for you.' ²⁹And when

she heard it, she got up quickly and was coming to Him. ³⁰Now Jesus had not yet come into the village, but was still in the place where Martha met Him. ³¹Then the Jews who were with her in the house, and consoling her, when they saw that Mary got up quickly and went out, they followed her, supposing that she was going to the tomb to weep there. ³²Therefore, when Mary came where Jesus was, she saw Him, and fell at His feet, saying to Him, 'Lord, if You had been here, my brother would not have died.'"
John 11:11-32

Again Jesus' faith is displayed when He told His disciples of His intention to awaken Lazarus from death for the glory of God. There is another aspect to suffering that I'd like to pause here to point out: both Martha and Mary cried out to Jesus in their grief by saying, "Lord, if You had been here, my brother would not have died." They were clearly grieved by the death of their brother, but felt such a close relationship to Jesus that they felt free to cry out to Him in their suffering. But when Jesus asked them if they trusted Him, they affirmed they did. So they experienced suffering, cried out to the Lord, but never doubted who He is. Let's continue reading John 11.

"³³When Jesus therefore saw her weeping, and the Jews who came with her also weeping, He was deeply moved in spirit and was troubled, ³⁴and said, 'Where have you laid him?' They said to Him, 'Lord, come and see.' ³⁵Jesus wept. ³⁶So the Jews were saying, 'See how He loved him!' ³⁷But some of them said, 'Could not this man, who opened the eyes of the blind man, have kept this man also from dying?'"
John 11:33-37

Even though Jesus had already spoken of His intention to raise Lazarus from death, He was "deeply moved in spirit" and "troubled" by the grief expressed from everyone. Furthermore, verse 35 is simple and straightforward: "Jesus wept." Why would He weep if He knew what was about to happen? It is my opinion that Jesus wept because of His love for all of them. Isn't that a beautifully sweet aspect of Jesus' character? Even though He was about to cure their mourning by raising

Lazarus, He still had the tenderness and care for these people to weep and grieve with them. This is a wonderful reminder that God truly sees and cares about every tear you shed. His heart aches when yours does. If you are a parent, you can probably relate to this feeling of your heart aching when your child gets hurt. He is all-powerful and all-knowing, yet He chooses to be a loving and tender Dad instead of a cold and distant Father who just performs miracles without caring about His people.

The onlookers had divided reactions to His weeping: some said it showed how much Jesus loved Lazarus, while others doubted Him and questioned why Jesus did nothing to stop Lazarus from dying in the first place. Haven't we all heard or thought ourselves why God allows terrible things to happen in this world and that if He is so powerful, why doesn't He stop suffering from happening? But remember that the whole purpose of this suffering was meant to bring glory to God. And now there was a large audience at Lazarus' tomb.

"38So Jesus, again being deeply moved within, came to the tomb. Now it was a cave, and a stone was lying against it. 39Jesus said, 'Remove the stone.' Martha, the sister of the deceased, said to Him, 'Lord, by this time there will be a stench, for he has been dead four days.' 40Jesus said to her, 'Did I not say to you that if you believe, you will see the glory of God?' 41So they removed the stone. Then Jesus raised His eyes, and said, 'Father, I thank You that You have heard Me. 42I knew that You always hear Me; but because of the people standing around I said it, so that they may believe that You sent Me.' 43When He had said these things, He cried out with a loud voice, 'Lazarus, come forth.' 44The man who had died came forth, bound hand and foot with wrappings, and his face was wrapped around with a cloth. Jesus said to them, 'Unbind him, and let him go.' 45Therefore many of the Jews who came to Mary, and saw what He had done, believed in Him."
John 11:38-45

If you also believe in Jesus, then you too have been unbound and let go of the tomb of sin. Your freedom from sin is every bit as great of a miracle as the raising of Lazarus from the dead.

⁓✦⁓

One day I realized that I was over a week late for my period to start. At that time, we had been married for three years, but we did not feel ready to have a child yet, so we were still using protection. We lived in a one bedroom/one bathroom apartment with five pets – yes, *five*! – and had just reached a point where we were both working full-time after grad school. We also were very squeamish around kids. I was an only child and did not babysit much, and Michael was the youngest and had no experience with kids. And when we were around kids, we seemed to always catch "the plague" because they seemed to be oozing from every orifice. We still wanted to have kids someday, just not for a while.

Michael also had some very selfish viewpoints about having children. The story he most likes to share as an example of this was when we were out eating lunch with a group of friends. The topic of breastfeeding came up (that's a normal lunch time topic, right?), and Michael shared with the group that he was not going to want me to breastfeed our future children because he didn't want to compete with a baby for my body. And having always valued health and physical appearance, he had also told me that he did not want me to gain much weight if I were to get pregnant. Him expressing that concern made me struggle for years with self-confidence regarding how he perceived my body.

So, when I realized that my period should have started over a week ago, I became really nervous about possibly being pregnant. We used protection, so how could this have happened? Well, I guess if it could happen to Rachel Green on *Friends*, maybe the same thing could happen to us? For some reason, instead of taking a home pregnancy test, I went to the doctor to have them do a blood pregnancy test.

I remember fretting all afternoon waiting for the phone call with the results of that test. How would we afford a baby? Would we have to move now, throwing off our plans of saving for a house? Would Michael still find me attractive after having a baby?

When my phone rang, I hesitantly answered. The nurse said, "Hi, I'm calling with the results of your pregnancy test…it was negative." Then something happened that I really wasn't expecting – my heart sank. I was…disappointed. Disappointed that I was *not* pregnant.

Over the next few weeks, that disappointment took root as a desire to become a mom. I remember feeling surprised to suddenly have this desire, and so I credited the Lord with placing it in my heart. In the months that followed, that desire grew and grew.

I communicated my desire to Michael, and we had several conversations about it. He still didn't feel comfortable moving on to that next chapter yet because he was concerned about how to afford a baby and feared the stress it would cause in our lives. Trying to be respectful of his feelings, I turned to prayer a lot. I prayed almost every day for Michael to feel comfortable and that the Lord would guide us in building a family. I had no idea at the time what was in store for us.

❧

One morning, seven months later, I attended a ladies cookie baking social while the husbands played flag football. The hostess of the cookie baking social had twin girls who were less than one year old at the time. At one point, she asked if I wanted to hold one of her daughters and feed her a bottle. I accepted the offer, and I remember thinking as I held that sweet, delicate little baby girl, "This isn't so scary…I could do this."

Later that morning, when our husbands came over to pick up their wives, I remember Michael held one of the twin girls too. It struck me in that moment how much I enjoyed the sight of my husband holding a baby. I definitely had a case of baby fever!

Later that day, Michael and I again had a conversation about starting a family, only this time, the conversation ended with Michael agreeing that it was okay with him if we started trying. I couldn't contain my excitement at that change in his decision!

I was delighted when Michael finally agreed that it was okay for us to start trying. But at the time, I thought that was all there was to it – just a decision couples make and then pregnancy would surely follow. After all, wasn't that the message in sex-ed classes growing up? Thou shalt use protection lest you *will* get pregnant...like it's a certainty, a cause-and-effect relationship.

We stopped using protection, and I began immediately planning for announcing our pregnancy later that month on Christmas morning. It was going to be a momentous occasion. My parents, my Meemaw, and Michael's mom (Lisa) would be *so* excited to hear our news! My mom would make a joke about becoming a Granny. Lisa would tear up with joy, hug us, and begin excitedly planning what to buy for the baby and us. My Meemaw would sweetly hug me and congratulate us. And my dad would silently process this change in his reality that his only daughter was going to have a baby of her own.

But five days before Christmas, I started my period. I was shocked to say the least. I mean, we did everything necessary to create a baby. In my mind, it was a simple formula to follow, so where did we go wrong?

Thinking that we must have simply missed my ovulation day for that month, I tried not to be discouraged. I searched the Internet for ovulation calculators and made sure I knew the proper formula and timing information. Next month it would *surely* happen. But then I started my period again the next month. And the next. And the next.

My heart started to sink over those first few months. The thought kept trying to creep into my mind, "What if you're going to have trouble getting pregnant? What if you're *never* able to get pregnant?" Not at all prepared to face those questions, I fervently pushed them away and buried them deep down and out of sight. Nope, those questions were *not* applicable to me. That was *not* going to be my story.

In the months that followed, my Control Mode went into hyper-drive. I read books about the fertility awareness method and trying to conceive. I joined online forums and began using all those silly acronyms to try to find out what we were missing. I created an Excel file to track every detail of my cycles to have data to analyze and learn from. I created a schedule – yes, a schedule – for when Michael and I should have sex.

If you're a married or will-be-married woman, please trust me when I say that this was a terrible thing to do. You may think that a guy is happy to have sex whenever and however often you demand, but that is not the case if you are only using him to try to create a baby. My husband always delighted in sex – except when I took all the fun out of it by being more interested in this potential child creation than in him. I treated him in this terrible way for a few months before I felt convicted about this wrong mindset.

It was around the six-month mark of trying to conceive that Michael and I had a needed conversation about our sex life and how much I was hurting our marriage by having tunnel vision about creating a baby. It had also been long enough of trying to conceive that I felt it was worth seeing a doctor to begin some basic diagnostic tests to see if anything could explain our lack of conception.

I visited my OB-GYN doctor shortly after and had some basic blood work taken. Everything came back normal, and the doctor said that it appeared that I was ovulating regularly, but recommended that I begin taking Clomid anyway. I didn't feel comfortable with that recommendation because Clomid was meant to stimulate ovulation – something that I was already doing, and I didn't want to take unnecessary medication. I felt frustrated with this doctor and her recommendation, so I determined that I would take a short break and find a new OB-GYN doctor once my new insurance plan began a couple months later.

❧

Remember that you cannot avoid suffering. You can't find yourself in the middle of suffering and then hit the escape button and say, "Okay, that's it, I'm ready to be done!" (Believe me, I have tried...)

But you can choose to be an example to others around you, believers and non-believers alike. Since you cannot control the circumstances of your suffering, focus on the things you do have control over: how you respond to your suffering. Remember that the eyes of the world are on you. Like Jesus at Lazarus' tomb, you may have a larger audience watching you than you realize. Your suffering may provide a wonderful opportunity to point to the glory and trustworthiness of God.

It is also important to understand that suffering well does not mean you put on a fake smile and pretend to be *happy* about your suffering. No, that would make you delusional and insane. It's perfectly okay and expected of you to feel sadness or grief as you suffer.

If we look to Christ's example of how to experience suffering, we see that He wept and felt grief because of His suffering, but He trusted God throughout it all. When facing death on a cross He agonized over the impending pain and suffering of that experience, crying out to God the Father, "Father, if You are willing, remove this cup from Me; yet not My will, but Yours be done." Therefore, you too should have complete faith that God is with you, cares for and loves you, and that He is still good.

"Therefore humble yourselves under the mighty hand of God, that He may exalt you at the proper time, casting all your anxiety on Him, because He cares for you."
1 Peter 5:6-7

We know that suffering is inevitable but has a purpose to bring glory to God. Suffering is not useless. It's an opportunity to share God's love and goodness with the world and for God to build your character.

"²Consider it all joy, my brethren, when you encounter various trials, ³knowing that the testing of your faith produces endurance. ⁴And let endurance have its perfect result, so that you may be perfect and complete, lacking in nothing."
James 1:2-4

"³And not only this, but we also exult in our tribulations, knowing that tribulation brings about perseverance; ⁴and perseverance, proven character; and proven character, hope; ⁵and hope does not disappoint, because the love of God has been poured out within our hearts through the Holy Spirit who was given to us."
Romans 5:3-5

God will use your suffering to grow you if you let Him. Suffering isn't easy, but just as suffering has a beginning, it also has an end. It may not end when or how you desire or plan, but it will end someday, somehow. You have hope.

"¹⁰After you have suffered for a little while, the God of all grace, who called you to His eternal glory in Christ, will Himself perfect, confirm, strengthen and establish you. ¹¹To Him be dominion forever and ever. Amen."
1 Peter 5:10-11

CHAPTER 3

What is Joy?

A few years ago, Michael and I traveled on a Mediterranean cruise for two weeks. At times it was a culture shock. For instance, if you have to use a restroom while in public, good luck finding one! They're well-hidden, and you're expected to buy something from a store or restaurant in order to have access to their facility. But for the most part, we had a lot of fun seeing so many different places.

Our disembarkation port was in Rome. We had about six hours between the time of getting off the ship and needing to be at the airport in Rome. We wanted to do a little bit of sightseeing during this window of time, so we took the cruise shuttle bus into the city to a train station. Because we were trying to save money, we packed light enough for this trip such that we only had carry-on luggage. Don't be too impressed – our carry-on luggage was stuffed *full* and was pretty heavy. We had heard before going on this trip that you can leave your baggage at the train station for a small fee and then pick it up later (baggage consignment). When the cruise shuttle bus dropped us off at the train station, we were expecting to utilize this service and then begin sightseeing. But when we walked into the train station, all the service windows were closed.

Confused and frustrated, we finally discovered by checking GPS maps on our phone that we were at the wrong train station – we needed to be at the Roma Termini station. To this day, I cannot tell you what train station we were at…I just know it was not the right one. So, we used the kiosk in the station (because there was no one available to help us) to figure out how to buy tickets from whatever station we were standing in to the Roma Termini station. We hauled our luggage up to the station platform and took the train to Roma Termini.

Upon arriving at this bustling and open station, we found the location of the baggage consignment service – and it had a line out the door and around the corner. As heavy as our luggage was, we had no choice. We had to offload our luggage if we were to have any hope of sightseeing that day. You were supposed to go to the kiosk near the front of the line to get a number and then go to the back of the line and wait until your number was called. The expected wait time was *hours*. As I was fiddling with the kiosk to get a number, praise the Lord that some kind soul got tired of waiting and handed me their number, which was a much smaller number than the one I just got from the kiosk.

We waited for about one hour in line to consign our baggage instead of multiple hours. The downside was that after the ordeal of being dropped off at the wrong train station and waiting to offload our luggage, we had only about four hours left to sightsee in Rome. For those unfamiliar with Rome, four hours is not much time at all. So we picked places that were within walking distance of the train station and that we were most interested in seeing. We ate lunch at a local restaurant and went to the Spanish Steps, Piazza Navona, Pantheon, Trevi Fountain, and lastly, the Colosseum.

The weather was sunny when we began our walking adventure but grew more and more overcast as we went along. By the time we were waiting in line to get into the Colosseum, it was lightly sprinkling. But it was a big deal that we were even able to get inside the Colosseum, given that we bought tickets right before getting in line. We think the ominous weather encouraged many tourists to not bother going to the Colosseum that day.

We were able to get inside and marvel at this historic landmark. And then thunder began building, and it started pouring rain. We found ourselves in the middle of a thunderstorm inside the Colosseum.

Now, depending on your attitude, you could have bemoaned this thunderstorm as ruining your sightseeing plans. A literal raining on your parade of Rome. But instead of being upset by the foul weather, we chose to see this as a one-of-a-kind opportunity in life. How often do you get to take shelter under the archways of the Colosseum during a thunderstorm? How often do you get to hear the reverberations of thunder echoing off the majestic walls that have withstood over 1,900 years of history? How often do you get the opportunity to laugh with your spouse as you squeal like a girl (just me of course) when the cold rain hits the back of your neck?

Life is made up of a series of choices you make. Of course not everything is within your control, but your attitude always is.

As mentioned in the previous chapter, suffering well does not mean that you pretend to be happy about experiencing suffering. Sadness is a normal and healthy response to pain and suffering. How can a person "consider it all joy...when you encounter various trials" as stated in James 1:2?

For many years I could not understand this verse from James 1. Joy when you encounter various trials? I used to think that meant that I should put on a smile and will myself to be happy when tough things happen. But can you imagine if that were actually what this verse meant? People smiling and acting happy while they bury a loved one, watch their marriage fall apart, lose their job, or any other myriad of heartaches that could happen? No, that would be insanity. Grief is not meant to be hidden or never experienced. A facade of happiness is not the same thing as experiencing joy.

In other words, joy does not equal happiness.

"¹Therefore, since we have so great a cloud of witnesses surrounding us, let us also lay aside every encumbrance and the sin which so easily entangles us, and let us run with endurance the race that is set before us, ²fixing our eyes on Jesus, the author and perfecter of faith, who for the joy set before Him endured the cross, despising the shame, and has sat down at the right

hand of the throne of God."
Hebrews 12:1-2

These verses describe Jesus and say that He, "for the joy set before Him endured the cross." I think it's safe to say that Jesus did not feel happy while enduring the torture of a death by crucifixion. In fact, in the Garden of Gethsemane Jesus was "deeply grieved" (Matthew 26:38) and "in agony" (Luke 22:44) and asked God to "remove this cup from Me" (Luke 22:42). He felt agony and grief, but He was joyfully obeying God the Father's will. Despite his feelings, He *chose* to still trust God and His Goodness. He *chose* to trust God's plan for Him. Choosing to trust God was something I really struggled with in my journey.

❧

During the same summer that I visited my OB-GYN and decided to take a little break from trying to conceive until I could switch to a different doctor in the fall, we began having our first house built. We had paid off all previous debt (student loans and a new car) and saved for a decent down payment. For years it had been our dream to build a house some day. We couldn't believe that we were actually getting to fulfill that dream in our *first* home!

We loved the builder that we were working with. He took us to see each of the potential lots to build on in the neighborhood, even though we had told him that this neighborhood was just out of our price range. But when we first walked onto the lot that would one day hold our house, I just had this feeling of "this is home" that I couldn't shake off. A few days later, my parents offered to loan us some money – it was enough to help us afford to build in this neighborhood, on the lot that already felt like home.

With that generous gift, we committed to our builder and began finalizing the details of the floor plan. Michael thrived in this environment because he loves digging into the details of home building. I certainly cared about it too, but I remember reaching my limit when I sat through a two-hour conversation about the kitchen built-in trash can. I told him that as long as we *had* a trash can in the kitchen, that's all I cared about and I'd be waiting in the car. But overall, building a house together was a really fun experience. We excitedly drove to our lot almost every day to see what new progress had been made.

When the house was framed up, we thought it would be a neat idea to write Scripture on the walls. We even invited family over to write verses with us. Because we were just starting to face infertility, I specifically chose verses that related to persevering through trials and waiting on the Lord. I wanted those verses to surround me in our new home, even if I could no longer see them once the drywall was installed.

Once we were moved in and settled in our new home that fall, I began thinking about which OB-GYN doctor to change to. I had already scheduled an upcoming appointment with a doctor and then later asked some friends for their recommendations. One recommended doctor sounded like she would be a good match for me, but I was feeling a bit overwhelmed with the decision of whether to switch my appointment to this newer recommendation or not.

One night I was praying and fretting about this decision that should not have been causing such anxiety, but I eventually stopped myself and realized: *Wait, God knows what's best. I should trust him with this decision.* I asked for a very specific sign: to see or hear the name Amy the next day (Amy was the first name of the doctor I was considering switching to). I remember feeling almost an instant sense of peace in having trusted the Lord with that decision.

The next day was Sunday, and in the rush of getting ready for church, I temporarily forgot about the previous night's prayer. While driving to church we were following behind a car for a good while that had a bumper sticker that said "Vote for Amy." I don't remember seeing what campaign this bumper sticker was advertising for, and I have never seen it again anywhere to this day. For some silly reason at the time, my brain did not connect this visual observation of the bumper sticker with my prayer request from the night before. It wasn't until I was talking with a friend after the church service that my memory pulled up the image of that bumper sticker from the morning drive. I'm sure my friend wondered why I suddenly tuned out of our conversation, but I couldn't help it. In that moment, I felt such a sweet sense of love from my sweet, Heavenly Dad. He literally answered my prayer the next day, not because He had to, but because He wanted to. Not all prayer requests result in such a clear or immediate response, but sometimes they do. Sometimes parents like to give good gifts to their children.

I went to that appointment a few weeks later, and it was a great visit. This new doctor was very respectful and sympathetic. She explained my options and asked what I wanted to do, rather than pushing a recommendation on me. (Shouldn't all doctors behave this way?!) At the time, we had only been trying to conceive for one year, and having had it confirmed with this new doctor that Michael's numbers and my blood work, cycles, and anatomy looked normal, we decided to keep trying and hoping that we might conceive naturally.

But this was just the beginning of my journey with infertility. I was about to discover how much my *feelings* affect my *attitude*.

❧

The next entire year was probably my darkest year of our struggle with infertility, and arguably of my life. It was the year that I felt like I was stuck riding a roller coaster – and due to a traumatizing experience as a child of getting stuck on a roller coaster, I *hate* roller coasters! Like the tide rising and receding on a sandy beach, I seemed to waver between a positive, glass-half-full and despairing, hopeless mentality. My feelings were all over the place.

I remember feeling forgotten and left behind, forced to

stand still in life while it seemed everyone else was free to move on to the next chapter of life that I so desperately wanted to join: parenthood. I remember numerous friends announcing their pregnancies. I eventually became very attuned to these announcements before they were announced. I could just tell by the couples' micro-expressions and body language what they were about to share. They usually gave one another *that look*, as if to communicate, "Oh darling, can we *finally* share with the world?!" Although I was genuinely happy for their news, I was even more heartbroken and distraught that my womb remained empty. Every time I logged onto social media, I was afraid that I would see yet another ultrasound or adorably clever pregnancy announcement picture. Another reminder of what I *didn't* have.

I remember feeling broken and like a failure in every way. I felt like a weird freak. What was wrong with me? Why was this so hard? Was there something more seriously wrong with me that the tests missed, like a hidden condition or cancer?

It's a popular quote that "comparison is the thief of joy," and I can attest to the truth in that bit of wisdom. At the time, I felt surrounded by pregnant women and young moms. I even had dreams (rather, my nightmares) about scenarios like that, where I was standing with a group of women and was the only one *not* pregnant. When I would go out in public, I seemed to always notice pregnant women, babies, and baby products. Instead of choosing to recognize the sweetness of a candid moment between a mother and her child, I only saw a painful slap in the face that I couldn't have my own moment like *her*. My mind would flood with lies from the enemy every time: *I bet she would complain about how tired that child makes her feel. What's so great about her that made her deserve a child and I don't? I'd make a better mother than her.* On and on with such ugly, misconstrued lies.

Movies and television were also inundated with pregnancy and motherhood – pregnancy is a popular Hollywood plot twist it seems. There were even special reserved parking spaces at the grocery store for expectant mothers. (A bitter thought I would think is, "Oh of course, the delicate pregnant woman needs special treatment. It would be such a tragedy for her to have to *walk* too far!")

Mother's Day felt very shameful and isolating, as if I wore a scarlet letter branding me as *infertile*. At our church, they do the traditional "standing of the mothers ritual," which made me feel so sad and left out. All I wanted to do was have the right to stand alongside them.

Baby showers were painful to attend because I again felt so isolated and sad, just wishing I could be in her shoes. I felt like I was drowning in despair and was powerless to stop it. I felt incapable of being happy for my friends and even stopped spending time with some friends who were pregnant or had babies because I could no longer enjoy the friendship.

During this dark year, I did not feel close to God. He seemed so distant, as well as cruel and uninterested in me. (In case you haven't caught on yet, I was very self-focused this year. It was all about *me*!)

I questioned His plan and His character. I wondered what I had done to deserve such cruel punishment. Honestly, I also wondered what others had done so well to deserve a baby. I questioned my right to call myself a woman if my body couldn't even do what it was created to do. Talk about a misplaced sense of worth! I blamed myself for having sinned in the past, thinking that this painful trial was what I deserved.

I seethed in anger when I would hear insensitive comments ("Just relax! It'll happen!" or "I know what you mean…it took us three whole months to get pregnant with our fourth child!") or complaints from friends about the "difficulties" of pregnancy or motherhood. Didn't they realize that I would have done anything to be able to vomit because I was pregnant or be tired all the time because I had a newborn? I turned green with envy when someone would say getting pregnant was so easy or they "weren't even trying."

Joy was not at all on my mind at that time. Feelings of sadness overshadowed feelings of happiness, and my attitude followed suit. I allowed bitterness to take root in my heart, and

I provided steady access to light and sustenance, letting it grow. This bitterness resulted in my inability and unwillingness to invest in friendships with young moms or pregnant friends. I stopped attending baby showers and had no interest in meeting the newborns that friends had. It all just hurt too much. And because I had such a skewed view of God, I was alone in my pain and relying on my own strength to get through it – and as you can see, my strength was severely lacking.

As I continued to try to withstand all of this pain on my own, I eventually began struggling with depression. I had no idea who I was, what the point of my life was, and where my true worth came from. I felt so exhausted with it all. It felt so unfair that so many other people in this world can have children with such ease. Every month I would have an ounce of hope that maybe that would be our month. I would read into every little twinge and possible early pregnancy symptom. I would try to patiently wait the two weeks until I could take a pregnancy test and then hold it under the brightest light and squint my eyes to try to see if maybe there was the faintest of a second pink line on the test strip. When my period would start, I was devastated every time and usually ended up sobbing, snot and all, in a fetal position in my closet. Why the closet? I really can't say...perhaps it just felt safe.

❧

Trusting God during hard times does not mean you have to act happy. Being joyful is a choice or a state of mind, whereas happiness is a feeling. And feelings are always temporary.

Likewise, sadness is a feeling. And it's okay to feel sad and to grieve when something painful happens. Jesus experienced grief when Lazarus died (John 11:35). But the key is to not let feelings dictate your attitude or state of mind and to not doubt God's love for you or His goodness.

In 2 Corinthians 11, Paul lists all of the forms of suffering and hardship that he endured in his years of serving Christ:

"²²Are they Hebrews? So am I. Are they Israelites? So am I. Are they descendants of Abraham? So am I. ²³Are they servants of Christ?—I speak as if insane—I more so; in far more labors, in far more imprisonments, beaten times without number, often in danger of death. ²⁴Five times I received from the Jews thirty-nine lashes. ²⁵Three times I was beaten with rods, once I was stoned, three times I was shipwrecked, a night and a day I have spent in the deep. ²⁶I have been on frequent journeys, in dangers from rivers, dangers from robbers, dangers from my countrymen, dangers from the Gentiles, dangers in the city, dangers in the wilderness, dangers on the sea, dangers among false brethren; ²⁷I have been in labor and hardship, through many sleepless nights, in hunger and thirst, often without food, in cold and exposure. ²⁸Apart from such external things, there is the daily pressure on me of concern for all the churches."
2 Corinthians 11:22-28

Despite all of these difficult circumstances, Paul was joyful and faithfully served the Lord. I like the book of Philippians as an example of Paul's joy. I encourage you to read the entire book, but here I will highlight several excerpts showing how Paul chose to be joyful and content in spite of all the suffering he experienced. And in case you did not already know this, Paul wrote the book of Philippians while in prison for preaching the gospel of Christ.

"[Ch. 1]³I thank my God in all my remembrance of you, ⁴always offering prayer with joy in my every prayer for you all...¹²Now I want you to know, brethren, that my circumstances have turned out for the greater progress of the gospel, ¹³so that my imprisonment in the cause of Christ has become well known throughout the whole praetorian guard and to everyone else, ¹⁴and that most of the brethren, trusting in the Lord because of my imprisonment, have far more courage to speak the word of God without fear... ¹⁸What then? Only that in every way, whether in pretense or in truth, Christ is proclaimed; and in this I rejoice.

Yes, and I will rejoice, ¹⁹for I know that this will turn out for my deliverance through your prayers and the provision of the Spirit of Jesus Christ, ²⁰according to my earnest expectation and hope, that I will not be *put to shame in anything, but that with all boldness, Christ will even now, as always, be exalted in my body, whether by life or by death. *[21]*For to me, to live is Christ and to die is gain...*

[Ch. 2][1]*Therefore if there is any encouragement in Christ, if there is any consolation of love, if there is any fellowship of the Spirit, if any affection and compassion, *[2]*make my joy complete by being of the same mind, maintaining the same love, united in spirit, intent on one purpose. *[3]*Do nothing from selfishness or empty conceit, but with humility of mind regard one another as more important than yourselves; *[4]*do not merely look out for your own personal interests, but also for the interests of others... *[13]*for it is God who is at work in you, both to will and to work for His good pleasure.*

[14]*Do all things without grumbling or disputing; *[15]*so that you will prove yourselves to be blameless and innocent, children of God above reproach in the midst of a crooked and perverse generation, among whom you appear as lights in the world, *[16]*holding fast the word of life, so that in the day of Christ I will have reason to glory because I did not run in vain nor toil in vain. *[17]*But even if I am being poured out as a drink offering upon the sacrifice and service of your faith, I rejoice and share my joy with you all. *[18]*You too, I urge you, rejoice in the same way and share your joy with me...*

[Ch. 3][7]*But whatever things were gain to me, those things I have counted as loss for the sake of Christ. *[8]*More than that, I count all things to be loss in view of the surpassing value of knowing Christ Jesus my Lord, for whom I have suffered the loss of all things, and count them but rubbish so that I may gain Christ, *[9]*and may be found in Him, not having a righteousness of my own derived from the Law, but that which is through faith in Christ, the righteousness which comes from God on the basis of faith, *[10]*that I may know Him and the power of His resurrection and the fellowship of His sufferings, being conformed to His death; *[11]*in order that I may attain to the resurrection from the dead.*

[12]*Not that I have already obtained it or have already become perfect, but I press on so that I may lay hold of that for which also I was laid hold of by*

47

Christ Jesus. [13]Brethren, I do not regard myself as having laid hold of it yet; but one thing I do: forgetting what lies behind and reaching forward to what lies ahead, [14]I press on toward the goal for the prize of the upward call of God in Christ Jesus. [15]Let us therefore, as many as are perfect, have this attitude; and if in anything you have a different attitude, God will reveal that also to you...

[20]For our citizenship is in heaven, from which also we eagerly wait for a Savior, the Lord Jesus Christ; [21]who will transform the body of our humble state into conformity with the body of His glory, by the exertion of the power that He has even to subject all things to Himself...

[Ch. 4][4]Rejoice in the Lord always; again I will say, rejoice! [5]Let your gentle spirit be known to all men. The Lord is near. [6]Be anxious for nothing, but in everything by prayer and supplication with thanksgiving let your requests be made known to God. [7]And the peace of God, which surpasses all comprehension, will guard your hearts and your minds in Christ Jesus.

[8]Finally, brethren, whatever is true, whatever is honorable, whatever is right, whatever is pure, whatever is lovely, whatever is of good repute, if there is any excellence and if anything worthy of praise, dwell on these things. [9]The things you have learned and received and heard and seen in me, practice these things, and the God of peace will be with you...

[11]Not that I speak from want, for I have learned to be content in whatever circumstances I am. [12]I know how to get along with humble means, and I also know how to live in prosperity; in any and every circumstance I have learned the secret of being filled and going hungry, both of having abundance and suffering need. [13]I can do all things through Him who strengthens me...

[19]And my God will supply all your needs according to His riches in glory in Christ Jesus. [20]Now to our God and Father be the glory forever and ever. Amen."

Excerpts from Philippians 1-4

I know that was a lot to take in at once, but hopefully you can see Paul's joyful attitude throughout the flow of the book. In Philippians 1, Paul shares how God has worked good into a seemingly bad situation. I'm sure Paul did not wish to be imprisoned, but God used Paul's imprisonment to lead several people to believe in Christ. Paul chose to be thankful for the opportunity and role he played in that situation instead of begrudging that he had been wrongfully imprisoned. Furthermore, Paul declared his desire that Christ be exalted in his body whether he was alive or dead. His greatest desire was for God to be glorified.

In Philippians 2, Paul reminds his fellow brethren that God is at work in us, for His good pleasure, and for His glory. He tells us that if we suffer hardship, it is best to respond without complaining because we appear as lights in the world to those watching us. I want to insert here that expressing sadness or grief during suffering is not the same as complaining. We know that it's not wrong to feel sad or to grieve because Jesus expressed both in His lifetime. But Jesus did not grumble or complain about His suffering. What Paul is pointing out here is that when people observe you suffering and you don't respond with complaints and bitterness, it is a perplexing reaction. Paul goes on to explain that his toiling and suffering was not in vain because God receives all the glory.

He elaborates on that idea in Philippians 3 by going so far as to say that he counts "all things to be loss in view of the surpassing value of knowing Christ Jesus my Lord." Wow, what a marvelous attitude to have in life! Literally his every breath and moment spent on earth was inconsequential to the value of being in relationship with Jesus. I also love the grace that comes through his words when he encourages his brethren to basically forget what's already in the past and keep reaching forward, pressing on toward the prize, which he says is the upward call of God. As someone who so easily gets weighed down by my own guilty feelings, I love how Paul reminds me to keep looking ahead, not behind me to what I can no longer change.

I also love how Paul had such a big picture view of his life. He kept his focus on his true purpose – pointing people to Christ – and not on the mundane or the day-to-day details. So often I allow a bad moment to pull my entire perspective into the mud. If I drop and break a glass in the kitchen, I will fume and grumble about being so careless for a ridiculous amount of time. But Paul reminds us to always keep a heavenly perspective. We are called for more. We are called for bigger purposes than we often dwell on. For a dose of even more grace, Paul reminds us that if we forget to have this heavenly perspective or attitude, ask God and He will reveal it to you.

Philippians 4 is perhaps more well-known than the previous chapters, but it's certainly worth going through still. Paul reminds us starting in verse 6 that a joyful attitude begins with gratitude. There is no easier way to change your attitude than to humble yourself and express thankfulness to God for something – for anything! There is always *something* to be thankful for.

I think a very close cousin to joy is contentment. Contentment is also a choice, not a feeling. But the good news that we get from Paul in this chapter is that contentment is something that he *learned*, which means that it's something we all can learn *through Christ*. I italicized "through Christ" because if you're anything like me, then you have often prayed Philippians 4:13 using this emphasis: *I* can do all things through Him who strengthens me. But after taking John 15:5 (*"I am the vine, you are the branches; he who abides in Me and I in him, he bears much fruit, for apart from Me you can do nothing."*) to heart, I realized that I needed to change my emphasis to: I can do all things *through Him* who strengthens me. I am merely the vessel through which Christ supplies all I could ever need. It's all about perspective.

So Jesus said to him, "Unless you people see signs and wonders, you simply will not believe."
John 4:48

Joy is choosing to believe God's Goodness even when there are no signs and wonders. Even when the answer is no. Even when you're forced to wait. Even when your circumstances are difficult. That choice is your path to joy and intimacy with the Lord.

Furthermore, the word "consider" in James 1:2 is "hegeomai" in Greek, which is also used in the Bible to mean "to rule, command, have authority over," as well as "to deem or think." Sometimes you may have to command your thoughts to look for God's Goodness in a painful situation. This supports the idea that you *choose* to be joyful rather than passively wait to *feel* joyful. You can choose to be joyful while simultaneously feeling sad.

Even if you can't understand why something painful has happened or you feel angry (another feeling), you are still capable *through Christ* to trust Him and have a joyful perspective about your suffering. I encourage you to not try to hide your feelings of sadness or convince yourself that it's wrong to feel sad when something painful happens. Allow yourself to feel sad for a time, but trust that God is using the experience for good somehow.

Jesus is your source of joy. Jesus is your source of contentment. Jesus is your strength, your sustenance, your endurance, your hope, and your everything.

"Now may the God of hope fill you with all joy and peace in believing, so that you will abound in hope by the power of the Holy Spirit."
Romans 15:13

CHAPTER 4
Empathy and Comparison

In case you haven't caught on yet, there have been just a few conflicts that have taken place in our marriage. What can you expect when two different people merge into one? In our case, we each have been *gifted* with the character trait of stubbornness. This steadily provides situations that are ripe for conflict.

How do you load the dishwasher? In my mind, there is only one way...my way (a.k.a. the right way)! Similarly, there is only one way to sort and fold laundry.

When it comes to cooking, Michael and I are pretty opposite. We both love food but primarily just the eating of it. The cooking part of the food experience is often a source of conflict for us.

I am the type of person who likes to cook from a recipe, with measured quantities and clear instructions to follow. I also like to take my time and clean up as I cook. The idea of cooking in a cluttered, messy kitchen makes me shudder. I also like to cook in silence or while listening to a podcast, but not too loudly.

Michael, on the other hand, sees a recipe as a suggestion. Like speed limits in Mexico. He also wants to cook as fast as possible so that he can move on to the next activity. Cleaning up along the way (or afterwards) is an obstacle to moving on, so he'll just leave it ~~for me~~ to do later. And he loves to turn some music on and have the volume loud enough for the neighbors to hear it.

Now, just because Michael wants to cook the opposite way I want to cook, does that make it the wrong way? Absolutely not! It's just different. Likewise, my way isn't wrong; it's just different. We've learned through the years to meet one another in the middle more or to compromise "our way" from time to time. But that didn't happen overnight – it took years for us to accept that our differences were not right or wrong, they are just different. Instead of comparing myself to him or competing with him, I learned to respect that our differences can be a wonderful thing.

❦

One of our favorite movies is *The Count of Monte Cristo* (starring Jim Caviezel). This story has so many themes to it, but one of them is hope. Edmond was young, naïve, in a loving relationship with Mercedes, and was best friends with Fernand Mondego. Edmond grew up poor; Mondego was wealthy. But Mondego struggled with discontentment – he was always jealous of Edmond and how happy he was, especially now that Edmond was with Mercedes because Mondego was also in love with Mercedes.

Mondego arranged for Edmond to be framed for a crime, which resulted in Edmond being sent to the worst prison in France: the Chateau d'if, an island prison with awful conditions. Edmond was flogged on the day he arrived and on each anniversary of his arrival day for 13 years. He could never leave his cell. He had to go to the bathroom in a wooden bucket that a guard would empty everyday through a slot in the door. He was fed only once a day a pitiful excuse for a meal.

At the beginning of his sentence, Edmond had hope that this imprisonment was a big mistake, and he would be rightfully released soon. His cell had the words "God will give me justice" carved into it, and for the first several years, Edmond continued to carve those words deeper and deeper. He had hope.

But over the years, his hope waned. He seethed with anger

toward Mondego and those who had betrayed him. But even that wasn't enough to keep him going. He tried to hang himself but was unsuccessful. He had zero control over anything in his life, even his desire to end it. He gave up hope.

But one day, he heard a strange sound coming from underneath him: a light tapping. He placed his ear to the floor to try to determine the source of the sound when suddenly the stone floor began to crack. Small cracks at first, then more as they spread. It was as if something was pushing from underneath. The stones finally broke apart and up arose a dirt-covered head. Edmond started to panic, wondering if perhaps he had died after all and was about to meet a demon or worse. But the head turned around and then shoulders and a body emerged. It was a man. Another prisoner.

In all of his years in prison, he hadn't seen or heard another person other than the guards who whipped and fed him. But suddenly, there was another person with him. A friendly old man, a former soldier and priest, who was called Abbe Faria.

The priest had been imprisoned longer than Edmond and never gave up hope. He had been digging a tunnel for years, hoping to escape, but had simply dug the wrong direction, digging deeper into the prison. But working together, they could dig in the other direction toward the outside wall. In exchange for Edmond's help, the priest offered to educate him and teach him how to fight.

His new friend gave Edmond hope again. Of course, Edmond was motivated by revenge, even though the priest tried to warn him that vengeance belongs to God and getting revenge wouldn't fulfill him. You can watch the movie to learn the details, but eventually Edmond realized the truth of that and recognized what really matters in life.

I know it's a fictional story, but I like how it shows an example of a person suffering, giving up hope, but then being encouraged to hope again by another person suffering in a similar way. The priest had suffered long before Edmond was ever in prison and was positioned and ready to speak truth and love into Edmond's heart.

This is the beauty of the fact that we never suffer alone. You are never truly alone. Not only is God always with you, but one of the reasons He allows His children to experience the brokenness and the pain of this world is so that we can encourage others along the way.

Even if you haven't experienced a similar type of suffering as a friend or loved one, you can still be an encouragement to them. You can still inspire them to hold onto hope.

A friend of mine had to bury two children that died late in two separate pregnancies. Though I wasn't present with her, I pictured her standing next to the grave each time, unable to stop the tears from falling as she watched her husband lower the tiny casket into the ground. I imagined her heart aching to the core and her mind racing with thoughts of why. I imagined her returning home later that day, still having to carry on normal activities and chores like an ordinary day, but in her heart, those days are forever tainted with grief. What could possibly be the reason for heartaches such as these? As someone who thankfully has not experienced her type of loss, I tried to encourage her in the only way I could: validate her feelings and encourage her to trust Christ and turn to Him for comfort.

This question is asked by many and in many different ways: "Why would God allow such terrible things to happen to those He loves?" I believe the simplest answer is *so that His glory can shine through*. How could terrible things result in His glory? Just as we were each created uniquely, our stories are each unique, with unique twists and turns and caverns along the way. But God is unlimited in His ability to redeem and shine through *any* circumstance.

I believe another reason why God allows terrible things to happen to those He loves is for the sake of building and strengthening community. When people surround you in your suffering, meet you where you are, accept you, love you, and walk alongside you, you are building your community. The body of Christ is strengthened, and ultimately, God gets the glory.

You can never truly know what it's like to experience someone else's pain, even if your own painful experiences or circumstances are similar. But you can allow yourself to try, to empathize with their pain by imagining how it feels to be in their shoes.

Empathy is seeing with the eyes of another,
listening with the ears of another,
and feeling with the heart of another.
Alfred Adler

Empathy comes naturally to some people and very unnaturally to others. But in either case, it's a loving, conscious choice to put yourself in someone else's shoes. And in our just-keep-scrolling-culture of not wanting to stop and think about things that are sad or uncomfortable, it is perhaps even more important to practice empathy.

Thankfully, we have the perfect example to follow: Jesus. Jesus was the embodiment of perfect empathy and compassion for those suffering.

"⁴⁰And a leper came to Jesus, beseeching Him and falling on his knees before Him, and saying, 'If You are willing, You can make me clean.' ⁴¹Moved with compassion, Jesus stretched out His hand and touched him, and said to him, 'I am willing; be cleansed.' ⁴²Immediately the leprosy left him and he was cleansed."
Mark 1:40-42

"When He went ashore, He saw a large crowd, and felt compassion for them and healed their sick."
Matthew 14:14

"²⁹As they were leaving Jericho, a large crowd followed Him. ³⁰And two blind men sitting by the road, hearing that Jesus was passing by, cried out, 'Lord, have mercy on us, Son of David!' ³¹The crowd sternly told them to be quiet, but they cried out all the more, 'Lord, Son of David, have mercy on us!' ³²And Jesus stopped and called them, and said, 'What do you

want Me to do for you?' [33]They said to Him, 'Lord, we want our eyes to be opened.' [34]Moved with compassion, Jesus touched their eyes; and immediately they regained their sight and followed Him."
Matthew 20:29-34

"[11]Soon afterwards He went to a city called Nain; and His disciples were going along with Him, accompanied by a large crowd. [12]Now as He approached the gate of the city, a dead man was being carried out, the only son of his mother, and she was a widow; and a sizeable crowd from the city was with her. [13]When the Lord saw her, He felt compassion for her, and said to her, 'Do not weep.' [14]And He came up and touched the coffin; and the bearers came to a halt. And He said, 'Young man, I say to you, arise!' [15]The dead man sat up and began to speak. And Jesus gave him back to his mother."
Luke 7:11-15

There are so many examples of Jesus seeing someone suffering with a disease, blindness, or loss and Him responding with compassion. In all of the miracles He performed, God always received the glory.

Even though you are not Jesus Christ, you can still follow His example by responding to suffering with compassion. You may not perform a miraculous healing in the same way, but God can use you to bring healing to someone's heart. God still receives all the glory.

Something I have learned through my own journey is that it is usually my painful experiences that allow me to relate to others and others to relate to me. The longer I live, the more varieties of pain I experience as the consequence of living in a broken world. But this has allowed me to more easily practice empathy and try to see the world through someone else's eyes.

"And immediately there fell from his eyes something like scales, and he regained his sight"
Acts 9:18

I know this verse relates to the moment Paul experienced

an encounter with Jesus, but I like the symbolism of a person who formerly could not see what was always in front of them suddenly being able to see clearly.

Through my own painful experiences, my eyes have been opened again and again. Even though I've had to experience pain to have my eyes opened, the truth is that I'm so thankful to finally be able to see. This is one of many reasons God allows His beloved children to experience suffering.

I would not go back and trade any of my painful experiences if I could. I would rather experience hurt and be able to see than live in a bubble and be blind. I love all that I've learned from my suffering. Of course there may be a few (okay, a lot of) tears shed along the way, but I will continue to be in awe of all that He is working out for good.

It's so easy to compare yourself to someone else, especially in a culture where people often post the best, happiest, most glamorous representation of themselves. Wishing you were a better parent, wishing you could look like them, wishing your job was as fulfilling as theirs, wishing that others were more like you...on and on. Comparing your particular journey to another's will do no good.

❦

After another year of trying to conceive (my dark year), we were still perplexed that there was no medical explanation for our infertility – "unexplained infertility," they call it. At almost two years into our infertility journey, we still did not feel comfortable trying fertility medications or treatments. We've seen God bless those methods in several friends, but for us, we just never felt peace about that route.

Having always been interested in staying healthy, we were intrigued to watch a documentary called *Forks Over Knives* recommended by some friends. After watching the main feature and the special features, we looked at one another and said, "Let's try this!"

Being the realistic planner that I am, we decided to wait to begin a one-month trial of this whole food, plant-based diet that the documentary talks about until after we returned from a trip to Boston. After living it up eating Italian food in the North End, we began eating a plant-based diet the day after we returned home.

We were certainly interested in trying this new diet in the interest of health (it has been shown to prevent and reverse heart disease, type II diabetes, and other common diseases in this country), but our main motivation was to see if it would help us conceive.

We felt hopeful. Maybe *this* was the missing link all along. Maybe God led us to this new diet and lifestyle in order to use it to allow us to finally conceive. But God had other plans. Although this new diet positively impacted my hormones and cycles, we still did not conceive. We did, however, each experience some major health improvements, such as weight loss, lowered cholesterol and blood pressure, cleared acne, digestive improvements, and less depression.

Much of following year was spent getting used to this new way of living and eating. I was also starting to experience a little bit of spiritual and emotional healing as I slowly surrendered little pieces of our struggle with infertility to the Lord. I stopped tracking my cycles on a daily basis and recognized that life only comes from God. This helped me not compare our journey to other couples' journeys – even if a couple "easily" gets pregnant, it has nothing to do with that couple; that life is a gift from God, not based on the couples' efforts. I started to focus on the concepts of hope and joy, slowly realizing that these were decisions, not feelings.

But this year was also a turning point in our marriage. One afternoon, I happened to notice some illicit Internet history on the computer. (Unlike in the past, I was not seeking to discover this, I just stumbled upon it.)

Instead of my old typical reaction of anger, judgment, and bitterness, God placed a new thought in my head that I really needed to hear: "Wow, it must be so hard to be a man who wants to be faithful and honor God in our sex-filled society.

Sex is everywhere you look; he must feel constantly bombarded with it." And then the most important realization hit me: "That's exactly like *me* feeling constantly bombarded with pregnancy and babies."

This newfound empathy for Michael led me to continue to reflect on how I struggled with jealousy and bitterness seemingly all the time, but I really wished that I didn't struggle with those things. I then put myself in Michael's shoes and thought about how I might feel if my spouse judged me and was embittered against me because of my struggles. That would have been so hurtful and made me feel ashamed and all alone in my struggle.

I remember telling Michael all of this later that afternoon, and it was a wonderful moment for our marriage. I asked for his forgiveness for having been so hurtful to him all those prior years, and he began letting go of his hurt feelings as he saw that I felt empathy for him. We were taking baby steps of trying to shove that elephant out of the room. It didn't heal everything right in that moment (elephants are quite heavy you know, so it can take a while to push them out of a room), but it was definitely the first step toward an intimate companionship that we had never had before.

❦

It is so true that comparison is the thief of joy – it only leads to feelings of inadequacy or superiority and nothing in between. Please understand that comparison is different from relating to or feeling empathy toward others. Comparison occurs when you discount or elevate your journey when thinking of another's journey. As if it's a competition and you're deciding who gets to come out on top. You either declare yourself as the winner or the loser.

"For we are not bold to class or compare ourselves with some of those who commend themselves; but when they measure themselves by themselves and compare themselves with themselves, they are without understanding."
2 Corinthians 10:12

The word "compare" in this verse comes from the Greek word "sugkrino," which means "to joint together fitly, compound, combine; to interpret; to compare." When I read this definition, I picture a scientist working on a project. The scientist is in charge, compounding, combining, and interpreting the elements he/she is working with. But contrast that verse and definition with this one:

"Therefore everyone who hears these words of Mine and acts on them, may be compared to a wise man who built his house on the rock."
Matthew 7:24

In this verse, Jesus uses the Greek word "homoioo" for "compared," which means "to be made like; to liken, compare; illustrate by comparisons." This definition reads more passive to me, like you're being molded or modeled after something good, rather than controlling the process. This verse encourages the reader to seek and imitate Jesus, who is the One doing the work in you, whereas the previous verse seeks to better oneself. In the former, you are the scientist in control; in the latter, you are the experiment under the control and guidance of Jesus, the loving Scientist.

When it comes to suffering, it can be easy for you to compare your experience to someone else's. Again, you will likely think one of two opposing thoughts: "I'm glad my suffering wasn't as bad as theirs" (inadequacy), or "They didn't suffer as much as I'm suffering" (superiority). Those kinds of thoughts only lead to self-centered thinking.

Comparing your specific suffering to another's will only steal your joy. Everyone's journey in life is going to look different. Even if the type of suffering is the same, we are each unique and respond to suffering in unique ways. Therefore, you will never have the same journey as another. Respect the uniqueness of each person's story. "Be quick to listen and slow to speak" (James 1:19). God gifts us uniquely, and He writes a unique story for each of us.

Can it be beneficial to relate to others about your suffering? Absolutely! It can be helpful to know others who have shared in similar types of suffering because they can offer encouragement and wisdom. But relating to others is very different from comparing your journey to another's. If you're not sure whether you're relating or comparing, the Holy Spirit will guide you if you ask Him to.

The surest way to maintain joy as you experience suffering is to abide in Christ.

"¹Therefore, since we have so great a cloud of witnesses surrounding us, let us also lay aside every encumbrance and the sin which so easily entangles us, and let us run with endurance the race that is set before us, ²fixing our eyes on Jesus, the author and perfecter of faith, who for the joy set before Him endured the cross, despising the shame, and has sat down at the right hand of the throne of God."
Hebrews 12:1-2

"¹Therefore if you have been raised up with Christ, keep seeking the things above, where Christ is, seated at the right hand of God. ²Set your mind on the things above, not on the things that are on earth. ³For you have died and your life is hidden with Christ in God. ⁴When Christ, who is our life, is revealed, then you also will be revealed with Him in glory."
Colossians 3:1-4

CHAPTER 5

Grace and Forgiveness

When I was maybe seven or eight years old, I attended a slumber party at a friend's house. There were a handful of other girls that attended. We played outside and played board games. As the evening of fun came to an end, we all started to get ready for bed. While a couple of us were brushing our teeth, I noticed that one of the other girls attending the slumber party was using baking soda as her toothpaste instead of a commercial toothpaste product.

I remember picking up the box and showing it to a few other girls, pointing out how strange it was to use that as toothpaste instead of using "normal" toothpaste like the rest of the girls. This poor girl whose feelings I had just hurt by making her feel like a weirdo began to cry. I immediately felt remorse. I apologized and tried to comfort her, and after a few minutes, she regained her composure and we made up. But still to this day, I sometimes feel guilty about treating her meanly.

I'm the type of person who has a really hard time letting go of guilt – for myself and unfortunately, sometimes for others too.

❧

I personally can think of no greater example in the Bible of grace and forgiveness covering guilt than in John 8 – the adulterous woman.

It was early in the morning, but Jesus was already in the

temple teaching lots of people. Then suddenly the temple doors opened and the scribes and the Pharisees walked in leading a disheveled young woman. Jesus and the people fell silent at the interruption and turned toward the newcomers.

The scribes and Pharisees were there to make a point, a spectacle. Stopping in the back of the crowd would not do. So they marched this young woman to the very center of the temple, so that everyone would have a clear view.

Then they said to Jesus, "Teacher, this woman has been caught in adultery, in the very act. Now in the Law, Moses commanded us to stone such women; what then do You say?"

The young woman's eyes dropped to the floor and her head lowered in shame. Heat rushed to her cheeks as she felt embarrassed and ashamed. There was nothing she could say. There was no misunderstanding. There was no mistake but her own. She was guilty.

Not saying a word, Jesus stooped down and began to write something in the dirt with his finger. The silence was deafening to the young woman as she awaited the grisly punishment she knew she deserved. Her heart pounded as the seconds passed.

Annoyed with His silence, the scribes and Pharisees pressed Him to respond. Jesus stood back up and said, "He who is without sin among you, let him be the first to throw a stone at her." Then He stooped down and began writing in the dirt yet again.

The young woman's heart skipped a beat as Jesus' words hung in the air. This must be it; surely a stone would come flying at her at any moment. She clenched her fists in anticipation of being pounded by stones.

But then one of the men walked away and left the temple. Soon after, another man exited as well. Then another and another. One by one the scribes and Pharisees left the temple until all had gone.

The young woman's eyes, still lowered to the ground, darted back and forth as her brow furrowed in confusion. She was too afraid to move. She blinked her eyes a few times to see if she was hallucinating. What had just happened, she wondered. Good Lord, it was so quiet.

Then Jesus stood back up and said, "Woman, where are they? Did no one condemn you?" She jumped a little at the sudden break in the silence of the room, but then quickly caught her breath as the kindness in his voice penetrated her heart. She slowly raised her eyes to meet Jesus'.

After pausing a few seconds, she replied, "No one, Lord." She held her breath, still not sure of what would happen next. Then Jesus, looking seemingly straight into her soul, softly and lovingly said, "I do not condemn you, either. Go. From now on sin no more."

The woman exhaled in relief and surprise. Tears began to fill her eyes as the weight of her guilt began to fall away from her shoulders, as the chains around her heart broke apart. Holding His gaze, she gave a small smile, the only way she could think to express her gratitude for the incredible gift Jesus had just given to her. She wasn't worthy of it. She was guilty, yet He forgave her. How could she possibly repay Him for such a gift? Somehow, deep in her heart, she knew she didn't have to. He wasn't asking her to. He just loved her and freed her. He saw the real version of her, the broken, sinful, ugly side of her, yet He forgave her. How marvelous, how wonderful is her Savior's love for her. And for you.

☙✿❧

When you're suffering, it is highly likely that people will say or do things (or sometimes fail to do things) that will feel hurtful and insensitive. I think it's common for a person who doesn't understand the pain you're experiencing to not know what to say or do to those who are hurting. And often times, people air on the side of caution and will choose to not say anything because they're afraid of saying the wrong thing. But sometimes the lack of saying something is more hurtful than saying something unhelpful.

It can feel overwhelming at times, no matter which side of the situation you're on. We live in a culture where people seem to get so easily offended that it can leave people confused and unsure how to be a good friend to someone struggling. This is why I think it's important to simply ask how you can be a good friend during their situation. Ask how you can pray for them. Ask about what would make them feel loved and supported during that difficult time.

It is my opinion that each person is going to judge differently what comments or actions are hurtful or insensitive. For example, a person who has just suffered the death of a loved one may want to be frequently asked how they're doing or talk about their lost loved one, while a different person in that situation may feel irritated by being asked and not want to talk about the person who died. One person grieving may prefer to stay busy and go back to their normal daily routine, while another person may prefer to be alone and process.

Just as each person is different in terms of how they handle a painful situation, people are likewise different in how they treat their friends who are experiencing pain. Again, some people are afraid of saying or doing the wrong thing, so they choose not to say or do anything, whereas some people are more likely to give advice on the situation, even if unsolicited.

Because we are all so different from one another, extending grace is a must. It is imperative for your heart that you choose to extend grace to people so that bitterness cannot take root.

"Be kind to one another, tender-hearted, forgiving each other, just as God in Christ also has forgiven you."
Ephesians 4:32

I encourage you to memorize and recite Ephesians 4:32 so that you are prepared for those moments where an extension of grace is needed.

❧

During my first three years of struggling with infertility, I cannot believe how frequently I had to extend (or more accurately *should have* extended) grace to others.

A woman struggling with infertility inevitably hears some fairly typical insensitive comments or questions:

- *"Do you have kids?"*
- *"So, when will you guys have kids?"*
- *"Just relax! It'll happen!"*
- *"Well, if it doesn't work out, you guys can just adopt a baby."*
- *"Have you tried [insert piece of advice, some of which is quite strange]? That worked for my sister."*
- *"Are you sure you're doing it right?"*
- *"Oh I know how you feel! It took us three whole months to conceive our fourth child!"*
- *"So why can't you get pregnant – is it his fault?"*
- *"Wow, I have no idea what that's like – all my husband had to do was walk into the room and I got pregnant!"*
- *"You should be glad you don't have kids yet – they're so exhausting! I mean, you guys can do whatever you want – vacations, date nights, whatever!"*
- *"Do you want to borrow one of my kids? Then I bet you'll be glad you don't have kids yet!"*
- *"Do you want to hold my baby to help you feel better?"*

I'm sure that list is not exhaustive, but you get the idea. In addition to the above typical insensitive comments, I encountered several situations where a hefty dose of grace was desperately needed.

On three different occasions (wearing three different outfits I should add), I was asked if I was pregnant. Out of the blue. One of the three times by a complete stranger at a store. Yeah...

In my defense, I know I was a little overweight before we began eating a plant-based diet but not overweight enough to warrant such bold questions. I'm pretty sure I never wore those three outfits again though, just in case...

One of the oddest and most grace-needed moments occurred at a work party that my husband and I attended. Michael and I both worked at the same company, and one night we attended a double-retirement reception in honor of two fellow co-workers. The reception took place in a hotel banquet room with light appetizer foods and alcoholic beverages for purchase. If only I could blame this upcoming scene on alcohol consumption, but alas, I cannot because this conversation took place shortly after the reception began.

There were lots of employees from our work that attended that evening: young, old, middle-aged, male, female, new employees, employees who have worked there for many years...get the idea? There were also some family members of the two retirees. It was your standard mix of people. Normal people.

But you know what happened to me? I was standing just behind Michael, who was talking to another co-worker. We were between the wall and a table – very much out of the way of the highly trafficked middle area of the room. Then I sensed that there was someone behind me, so I turned around. It was a middle-aged/older woman, who I later found out was also an employee at the company even though I had never met her before. The first words out of her mouth to me were:

Crazy Lady: "So, where's the baby???"

(Crickets chirping....to allow the similar moment of shock to hit you like it did me...)

Me: "What baby?"

Crazy Lady: "Your baby!"

Me: (Patting down my body and checking my pockets, just in case I missed something) "...I don't have a baby..."

Crazy Lady: "You don't have a baby?!"

Me: .....

Crazy Lady: "I'm looking for John's other son..."

Me: "Okay..."

Crazy Lady: "They have a baby."

Me: (Pointing across the room to a young woman who was actually holding a baby) "There's a baby..."

Crazy Lady: "Oh, I've already met her. She is John's other son's wife, that I've already met."

Me: "I'm sorry, I don't know how to help you..."

Crazy Lady: "Oh okay, well I'm [Name Withheld – my effort to extend grace to this crazy lady], and I work in Administration."

I introduced myself and Michael, who had turned around about the time that I pointed to the woman holding the baby, but then I just walked away. You just can't make this stuff up.

On the drive home, after again asking Michael if I looked pregnant (obviously I was very sensitive about this after being randomly asked three different times), I asked him, "Why does this type of thing keep happening to me? Seriously, why me? That could have happened to any other young-looking woman in that room; why did that have to happen to me?"

His answer was, "Because you're struggling." This reminded me of some truth.

"¹¹Put on the full armor of God, so that you will be able to stand firm against the schemes of the devil. ¹²For our struggle is not against flesh and blood, but against the rulers, against the powers, against the world forces of this darkness, against the spiritual forces of wickedness in the heavenly

places. ¹³Therefore, take up the full armor of God, so that you will be able to resist in the evil day, and having done everything, to stand firm."
Ephesians 6:11-13

"⁸Be of sober spirit, be on the alert. Your adversary, the devil, prowls around like a roaring lion, seeking someone to devour. ⁹But resist him, firm in your faith, knowing that the same experiences of suffering are being accomplished by your brethren who are in the world."
1 Peter 5:8-9

"He is Evil. I don't know how else to describe it. He is Evil, and like all evil, he has enormous power. He tempts. He taunts. And he takes."
Jonas in <u>Son</u> by Lois Lowry

Michael was completely right. It wasn't a simple coincidence that events like these kept happening to me. The enemy was using every opportunity he could scrounge up to steal my hope, faith, and joy – to get me to doubt God's goodness. If you are experiencing suffering, then you can be certain that the enemy is doing the same to you.

And what's most challenging is that all of the enemy's efforts are unseen physically. The enemy is working actively behind the scenes, under the radar, in secret, in disguise, in the darkness, and in the whispers of the mind, undetected and unrelenting.

Praise the Lord that He has conquered ALL! He has provided each and every person the opportunity to readily prepare for those battles where grace is needed. He freely gave His Son to allow us to have an eternal relationship with Him, to allow His Holy Spirit to live in our hearts to win the final battle no matter how you get there. Furthermore, He has freely given us His everlasting Word, the source of 100% truth, that has the ability to train us and teach us to put on the full armor of God. He gives us all the grace and forgiveness we will ever need to extend to people who hurt us.

Most people are not trying to hurt you (admittedly, some are, but this is likely rare). Remember that it is difficult for people to know what to say to someone who is suffering or hurting with something they have not experienced. But they mean well. It's important to give them the benefit of the doubt. They may say something that is the polar opposite of helpful, but their heart's intention is likely to comfort and show love to you. If you feel bold, you can kindly take the opportunity to help educate others about your experience and encourage them about what is helpful and supportive to say. But at the very least, remember to give them some grace.

☙✻❧

Having just said it's important to give people grace, I recognize that sometimes you have a relationship with a person who is intentionally hurting you or has a hardened heart. What I mean by hardened heart is that you have tried to explain why their words or actions about your suffering hurt your feelings, but the person still has not made an attempt to change how they treat you.

These types of hurtful relationships can come in all shapes and sizes. It may be a family member, acquaintance, or co-worker, which can complicate matters because you may be obligated to continue being around that person. If it's possible to see the person less frequently or not at all, that may be a simple way to protect yourself from being hurt. No matter your situation or the type of hurtful relationship, there are some key points to keep in mind.

"See to it that no one comes short of the grace of God; that no root of bitterness springing up causes trouble, and by it many be defiled"
Hebrews 12:15

[31]Let all bitterness and wrath and anger and clamor and slander be put away from you, along with all malice. [32]Be kind to one another, tender-hearted, forgiving each other, just as God in Christ also has forgiven you."
Ephesians 4:31-32

When someone has hurt you, you will likely face the temptation of bitterness. Bitterness can be thought of simply as a refusal to let go. If not careful, bitterness can take root in your heart and spread like poison throughout your body. I love how Hebrews 12:15 advises that everyone is able to receive the grace of God. As Ephesians 4:32 says, because Christ has forgiven you, you are called and able to forgive others. All believers in Christ are covered by His grace.

These two verses also warn against the consequences of holding onto bitterness. It will cause trouble in your life and defile many. I'm sure you can think of at least one person you know who you would describe as bitter. And you probably do not enjoy spending time with such a negative person.

Note in Ephesians that you must put bitterness away from you, or as I like to think of it, dig up the root of bitterness. Similar to joy, it's a choice you consciously make to expel bitterness from your heart. And like weeds in a garden bed, you have to constantly be on the lookout for new roots of bitterness that need to be dug up and thrown out.

If you feel overwhelmed with bitter feelings, I encourage you to pray to the Lord and surrender those feelings to Him to work through. He will provide healing and forgiveness if you trust Him with your pain.

I also want to distinguish between forgiveness and reconciliation. Forgiveness occurs when you no longer hold the offense over the offender's head. You have chosen to release the offender from their debt owed to you for their wrongdoing. Forgiveness only requires one person – you deciding to forgive. Reconciliation is a restoration of the relationship, continuing to pour in the resources of time and care to maintain the relationship. Reconciliation requires two people for the relationship to work well.

In some situations, it may be unhealthy to reconcile your relationship with the person who has offended you during your time of suffering. But it is always imperative that you let go of bitterness toward that person and choose to forgive them.

"To forgive is to set a prisoner free and discover that the prisoner was you."
Lewis B. Smedes

True forgiveness can only come from the Lord and His strength, not your own. Because humans are unable to literally "forgive and forget," we must trust God to bring forgiveness through us by living dependently on Him. It always starts with surrender – you must reach a moment (and you may have to repeat this moment again and again as you are reminded of the offense) where you surrender your pain to the Lord and trust Him to help you work through it.

In my own journey, I realized that I had wronged some friends through my bitterness and asked for their forgiveness. I also realized that I had a few friendships with people that were ultimately not healthy because they were unwilling to try to understand my pain or support me through it. I felt like my journey of suffering revealed which relationships were not grounded on a strong foundation. It took me many years to surrender the hurt feelings those people had caused me and to trust the Lord to bring forgiveness into my heart, but it was freeing once I made that choice. Refusing to forgive someone is actually most burdensome for you.

Whether someone intentionally or unintentionally hurts you, it is so important for you to let grace abound. You must accept the grace offered to you by Christ that will bring healing, strength, and forgiveness into your heart. You must also extend that grace outward to those who hurt you. Without grace, we are all imprisoned by sin.

CHAPTER 6
True Identity

Who am I? This question is one of the foundational questions that every human being in the history of time has faced and wrestled with. We all choose to identify ourselves in different ways based on our experiences and culture.

In Kindergarten, I made the decision that I did not like my full name "Christine" anymore but would instead like to be called "Christy." I wrote "Christy" on all my school work and would get angry if my parents forgot that I had changed my name and called me "Christine" instead. I remember thinking that "Christy" was such a fun-loving, easy-going, cool name. That's why I wanted it to be my name! I thought that by calling myself "Christy," I would suddenly transform into a cool, well-liked girl with tons of friends. I would no longer feel shy or awkward around my peers but would instead be charismatic, and other girls would desire to be friends with me.

Well, of course that didn't exactly play out the way I had envisioned. There was no overnight transformation when I showed up at school the next day and called myself "Christy." I had the same number of friends as I did the day before. I don't remember feeling more fun-loving, easy-going, or less awkward compared to when I called myself "Christine." Oh well, it was worth a shot.

Even this silly example as a Kindergartner reveals a very important truth in life: your behavior is a reflection of how you see yourself.

*"It is when we understand **who we are** that our behavior changes. Doing flows from being, not vice versa."*
Steve McVey, <u>The Grace Walk Experience</u>

"We all live by faith in someone or something. And everything that we are and do is a result of what we believe. Our behaviors are the tangible expression of our beliefs."
Jeff Vanderstelt, <u>Gospel Fluency</u>

I wanted to change my name to "Christy" because I believed that my full name "Christine" was boring and unlikeable. In essence, I was viewing myself as boring and unlikeable, so therefore my attitude and thoughts followed my core beliefs.

Steve McVey also shares that "Nobody consistently behaves in a way that is a contradiction of how he perceives himself to be. In other words, what you think about yourself will be the ultimate factor in determining the actions of your lifestyle."

For better or worse, your thoughts and behavior reflect how you perceive yourself. If you see yourself as worthless and unloved, then your mindset will habitually think like you are worthless and unloved. And you will likely behave in self-destructive ways, like basing your worth on what people think of you or how successful you are in life or becoming dependent on harmful substances or habits to name a few.

By my teenage years, I was already identifying myself based on my circumstances in life. At that age, what mattered most to me was what other people (especially boys) thought about me. As you can imagine, when you make your identity dependent on other people, the outcome is a very lost sense of self. I also did well in school but had a misplaced sense of identity in my accomplishments. This meant that if I received a grade below an A on anything, I felt devastated because it was as if the teacher was saying that *I* was below an A. School was hard enough without the extra pressure of my identity weighing on my shoulders!

Furthermore, I regularly identified myself based on my role in life. For many years in high school and college, I desperately wanted to have the identity of *Girlfriend*. When I began dating my future husband in college, I felt a sense of relief for having achieved the desired *Girlfriend* identity but was suddenly afraid all the time of losing that identity.

When we got married, I identified myself as *Wife*. I took this identity very seriously. When Michael would say something like, "Dinner tasted a little bland," I felt devastated because I instead heard him saying that I'm a bad wife, which was a direct attack on my very identity. I'm sure it's no surprise to you that there were many examples of conflict like this in our marriage due to my misplaced sense of identity.

My greatest struggle with identity arose when we made the decision to begin trying to conceive. I instantly upgraded my identity from *Wife* to *Wife AND Mother*. When months passed without getting pregnant, I really began to question who I was.

☙❀❧

As the year 2013 continued, so did my healing. I began to surrender more and more of our struggle and my desires to the Lord. I began to see how several good things had come as a result of our infertility. I had met several dear friends who also shared in the sisterhood of infertility. Our marriage had grown stronger. We had enough of an open-mind to change our diet and lifestyle for the betterment of our health and the environment. My faith was growing stronger and stronger as I reflected on all the good that God was bringing about from our pain.

I also began to experience healing about myself and my body. I realized that our infertility was no one's fault, certainly not caused by Michael's or my past sin. I also learned more about adoption from friends who had adopted, plus TV, movies, and books. I began to see examples of adoption more and more often. These examples were likely there all along, but for the first time in my life, I was taking notice of them.

Unbeknownst to me, the same realizations were occurring in Michael's heart.

In the early fall, Michael and I had a conversation that ended up on the subject of adoption. We then revealed to one another that we each felt comfortable with the idea of adopting. And unlike our conversations about adoption from a year prior – where we felt like we might be open to it after resolving our efforts to have biological children – we each expressed that our hearts had changed. We both felt comfortable with the idea of adopting now, whether we ended up having a biological child first or later (though I still was not willing to yield to the possibility of never getting pregnant). We were open to trusting God with the method and timing of bringing our future children into our family.

In the fall of 2013, we began searching for an adoption agency to work with. We tried to apply with a local agency, but they said they would add us to a waitlist because they would not be accepting new families for at least a year. Feeling discouraged at the potential long wait, we didn't know of a better option at the time. So we waited a couple months.

❦

At the beginning of 2014, we were enjoying re-watching the TV show *Friends*. We happened to be near the end of the series when Chandler and Monica were dealing with infertility and deciding to adopt a baby. We watched the episode where Chandler and Monica traveled to Ohio to visit a potential birth mother. It occurred to me, "Hey, they live in New York, but they were hoping to be matched with a birth mother living in Ohio. Surely there are larger adoption agencies than the local smaller ones we had looked at that might increase our odds of being chosen sooner." Again, God can work anywhere, right? He can even use a TV show to lead His children.

I remembered that a friend of mine, who was also hoping to adopt, had told me about an agency in our state. This agency was larger and would assign a caseworker to the adoptive parents and a separate caseworker to the birth parents. She explained the benefit of that was similar to having separate real estate agents – you want someone whose job is to just be in your corner.

I looked into this agency some more and saw that they place several hundred babies each year – much more than the local agency we were on a waitlist for. Wanting to learn more about the process of adopting with this agency, we signed up to attend their next orientation seminar in February. I remember that I was scheduled to work that day, and the seminar was only offered once a month. A very kind co-worker was willing to switch schedules with me so that I could have that day off, without me having to explain why.

At the orientation seminar, we felt nothing but peace. We also felt excited because it seemed like a great agency to work with, and it was exciting to have a potential path forward. We learned about the adoption process: applying and completing the home study, building your life book and profiles, the average wait time, the match process, and the steps to finalization. It was a lot to take in, but we felt like this was the agency for us to work with.

We submitted our application in March 2014. Unbeknownst to us, this was the month that our daughter was conceived.

❦

2014 was a year of highs and lows. For those unfamiliar with adoption, the process can be a bit overwhelming and invasive. First, there is a mountain of paperwork to fill out, including medical history, financial situation, and background checks. Then you go through the home study process where you are interviewed as a couple and individually. This is where it gets really *personal*, like all up in your business. They ask about your childhood, how you were raised by your parents (and any struggles you had), how you envision parenting and dealing with unmet expectations, and about your marriage (it's cohesiveness and conflicts).

Then you have to answer questions about your level of comfort and openness to the birth family, including contact with them after placement, ethnicity, medical history, drug/alcohol use, incest/rape, and special needs. It felt really uncomfortable thinking about all of those things, but we realized that it's important to be completely honest with where you're at, for the sake of the child. You don't want to say you're open to something that you're not really open to. I couldn't help but think that parents having biological children do not have to go through such an invasive process. After we completed our home study, we waited a couple of months for them to review our file to accept or decline.

The first low of the year came shortly after our seventh anniversary: we had to put one of our beloved cats to sleep. For non-pet people, this may not mean much to you, but for pet lovers, you know how devastating this can be. Fred (we also had a cat named Ethel; I've always been an *I Love Lucy* fan) was a great, cool cat. But he was prone to urinary blockages, which eventually led to pancreatitis, and it was clearly the right decision. But I definitely cried for weeks because Fred and Ethel had been with me since high school. I remember after we buried him in the back yard, I watched Ethel slowly walk to his gravesite, sit down, and give a sweet little meow as if saying goodbye.

Later in the summer, after a beautiful vacation to Costa Rica, we felt ready to adopt a new kitten. We named her Maddi and enjoyed her spunky personality.

In August, we heard from our adoption agency that we were officially accepted as a waiting family. They told us that from that point on, we could expect an average wait time of about 15 months. Next, we worked on our profiles and "Life Book." We were a little nervous about putting in our profiles that we eat a plant-based diet because we feared no birth mother (especially in Texas) would want to choose a couple of crazy, leaf-eating hippies to adopt her baby. But our caseworker encouraged us to be ourselves, and if it was important to us, then it's important to reflect our true selves. We posted our online profiles, made our photo "Life Book," and began the hopeful wait of being chosen by a birth mother.

But perhaps the most important thing that occurred that month was that I reached my final place of brokenness about our infertility. We never gave up hope that we still might conceive naturally. Strangely, Michael's sperm analysis had gotten a little worse over the years. And I still had painful and irregular periods. These ailments were still lingering even though we were so much healthier than we had been at the start of our infertility journey. Thinking perhaps that I had a thyroid issue, I went to an appointment with an ENT doctor in town.

This appointment went terribly and was the worst experience I've ever had with a doctor. He was pompous and disrespectful. He said that the reason I couldn't get pregnant was because I eat a vegan diet. (I snarkily thought, "Yeah, because you're the beacon of health. And oh yes, that must be it…because I was *so fertile* during those two years of infertility while eating meat. It must have just all been in my head.") There were several other condescending statements made to me in that appointment.

Once Michael and I got into the car, I broke down into tears. I was so sick and tired of feeling like I was broken. I made the decision to completely give up all efforts of trying to get pregnant. I just…quit. If God wanted to give us children, then He would. In His timing, and in His way, biologically or through adoption. I was done. I finally reached the point where I could say that if I never got pregnant, I would be okay. God would still be good. I decided to completely trust God to make us parents. Even though it was a dark moment, it was also incredibly freeing to "quit" and truly surrender this area to God.

That moment of brokenness was so critical for my spiritual well-being and sense of identity. I finally accepted that my identity was not based on my role or circumstances in life. God was good without my being a mother, and He would remain good if I later became a mother. I finally understood that my identity is grounded in who God is and what He says about me, not what I do or don't do. I finally understood that He sees me as His child, adopted into His family because of Christ. I am who I am, because of who Christ is and what He already did on the cross. Nothing can ever change that. No amount of success or failure, fortunate or unfortunate circumstances, and actions or inactions will change this identity.

A simple example of this truth can be found in the movie *The Lion King.* (Spoiler alert.) When Simba's father, Mufasa, died, Simba ran away because he felt guilty and ashamed that he caused Mufasa's death. Simba grew up, lived with Timon and Pumba, and refused to think about his past. But then Rafiki found him and took him to a remote clearing where Mufasa appeared to him in the clouds. Mufasa said, "Simba, remember who you are."

Simba's decision to run away, his refusal to think about his past, and the great distance he put between himself and his homeland – none of it changed his identity. He always was and always would be Mufasa's son. Simba just needed to realize that nothing changed in his identity. His identity wasn't based on his behavior, good or bad; it was based on being Mufasa's son.

The biblical example of this truth is found in Luke 15:11-32, The Prodigal Son.

"[11]And He said, 'A man had two sons. [12]The younger of them said to his father, "Father, give me the share of the estate that falls to me." So he divided his wealth between them. [13]And not many days later, the younger son gathered everything together and went on a journey into a distant country, and there he squandered his estate with loose living. [14]Now when he had spent everything, a severe famine occurred in that country, and he

*began to be impoverished. *[15]*So he went and hired himself out to one of the
citizens of that country, and he sent him into his fields to feed swine.
*[16]*And he would have gladly filled his stomach with the pods that the swine
were eating, and no one was giving anything to him. *[17]*But when he came
to his senses, he said, "How many of my father's hired men have more
than enough bread, but I am dying here with hunger! *[18]*I will get up and go
to my father, and will say to him, 'Father, I have sinned against heaven,
and in your sight; *[19]*I am no longer worthy to be called your son; make me
as one of your hired men.' " *[20]*So he got up and came to his father. But
while he was still a long way off, his father saw him and felt compassion
for him, and ran and embraced him and kissed him. *[21]*And the son said
to him, "Father, I have sinned against heaven and in your sight; I am no
longer worthy to be called your son." *[22]*But the father said to his slaves,
"Quickly bring out the best robe and put it on him, and put a ring on his
hand and sandals on his feet; *[23]*and bring the fattened calf, kill it, and let
us eat and celebrate; *[24]*for this son of mine was dead and has come to life
again; he was lost and has been found." And they began to celebrate.' "*
Luke 15:11-24

The younger son went off to a far away land to live for
himself. When he realized his folly, he decided to return home
and tell his father that he was no longer worthy to be called his
son. But did you notice the father's reaction? "But while he
was still a long way off, his father saw him and felt compassion
for him, and ran and embraced him and kissed him." Before
the son could even get his prepared speech out, his father had
already welcomed him back with a loving embrace and called
for a celebration. No matter what you've done, what mistakes
you've made, this is how God the Father sees you too. He's
always waiting by the window, squinting toward the horizon,
hoping to see His child return to Him…so that He can
welcome His child in a loving embrace.

But for all the perfectionists out there who struggle with
being "good enough," the story doesn't stop here.

"[25]*Now his older son was in the field, and when he came and approached
the house, he heard music and dancing. *[26]*And he summoned one of the*

servants and began inquiring what these things could be. ^{27}*And he said to him, "Your brother has come, and your father has killed the fattened calf because he has received him back safe and sound."* ^{28}*But he became angry and was not willing to go in; and his father came out and began pleading with him.* ^{29}*But he answered and said to his father, "Look! For so many years I have been serving you and I have never neglected a command of yours; and yet you have never given me a young goat, so that I might celebrate with my friends;* ^{30}*but when this son of yours came, who has devoured your wealth with prostitutes, you killed the fattened calf for him."* ^{31}*And he said to him, "Son, you have always been with me, and all that is mine is yours.* ^{32}*But we had to celebrate and rejoice, for this brother of yours was dead and has begun to live, and was lost and has been found."*

Luke 15:25-32

The older son had behaved well, had done all the right things, and now could not understand how his father could be so welcoming to his younger brother who had behaved so badly. It wasn't fair. But the father's response was, "Son, you have always been with me, and all that is mine is yours." In other words, the older son's status never changed. He was and would always be his son, no matter how good his behavior. Likewise, the younger son always was and would always be his son, no matter how bad his behavior. Both sons' identities were based on the father's view, not the sons' behavior. You are a child of God because He says you are, not because you did (or didn't do) anything to earn it.

The challenge of facing an identity struggle in a practical sense is that the enemy is a crafty, evil one who uses a variety of strategies to attack your mind and lead you away from trusting in God:

Strategy	Ways It's Used	Examples
Lies	About God and His goodness; often presented in the first person in your mind	"I'm worthless." "God doesn't love me."
Accuses	Covers you in shame; also often presented in the first person	"I failed, again." "I should have been better."
Tempts	Promises fulfillment in sinful pleasures; God's ways are too difficult	"Go ahead and do this. You work hard. You deserve this." "No one else will know." "You're already forgiven; you might as well enjoy yourself."
Divides and Isolates	Uses pride, bitterness, and contention to break community with others	"Ugh, this person deserves to hear the truth." "Everyone will think I'm so funny if I say this." "No one could possibly understand me, so I might as well keep this to myself." "I don't need anyone else."

*Adapted from Gospel Fluency, by Jeff Vanderstelt, chapter 8

Satan also isn't rigorous in how he uses these strategies. Oftentimes they will overlap and blend together (for example, he'll use a temptation in conjunction with an accusation). He has had thousands of years of practice and is masterful in these tactics.

What should you do if you realize that you are misplacing your identity in anything other than as a child of God?

"Be anxious for nothing, but in everything by prayer and supplication with thanksgiving let your requests be made known to God. And the peace of God, which surpasses all comprehension, will guard your hearts and your minds in Christ Jesus.

Finally, brethren, whatever is true, whatever is honorable, whatever is right, whatever is pure, whatever is lovely, whatever is of good repute, if there is any excellence and if anything worthy of praise, dwell on these things."
Philippians 4:6-8

In a practical sense, a way to apply these verses when you are struggling with your true identity is to develop the habit of identifying these strategies and counteracting them with Truth. This is the main reason why I created Mirror Ministry – so that you can always have Truth in front of you when you're battling with your thoughts in the mirror. You can learn more at mirrorministry.com.

I know from personal experience that it can take time to learn how to identify these strategies, but you will get quicker at it if you keep trying and asking God to reveal them to you and to help you take "every thought captive to the obedience of Christ" as 2 Corinthians 10:5 says.

For the lies especially, if you're not careful to identify them for the lies they are, then those lies over time will travel and take root in your heart. They can become your inner voice that you live trapped under, like you've fallen in a frozen lake and are fighting to break through the ice to get more air. But even if you have a lifetime's worth of lies buried deep in your heart,

God has already overcome the evil one, so do not fear. He can redeem and heal your heart. He has given you the Holy Spirit to whisper Truth in your heart when the evil one tempts you with a lie. Keep seeking His wisdom and discernment through prayer, reading His Word, and dwelling "on these things" in Philippians 4. It can also be helpful to physically write down the big lies you've believed in your heart and look up Scripture to counteract each lie with God's Truth. I'll show an example of this using some of the lies from the previous table:

Lie	Truth
"I'm worthless."	Psalm 139
"God doesn't love me."	John 3:16
"No one else will know."	1 Samuel 16:7; Hebrews 4:13
"You're already forgiven; you might as well enjoy yourself."	Romans 6:15
"I don't need anyone else."	Galatians 6:2; Proverbs 27:17

Another practical step you can take today – a very first step you can take on your journey to healing and believing your true identity – is to practice the art of gratitude. As Philippians 4:6 says, "but in everything by prayer and supplication with **thanksgiving**," gratitude is key. You could even make an Ebenezer ("stone of help"), which is a tangible reminder to give thanks to God for a time when He was Good or Faithful. You can always, always find *something* to be grateful for. Even if it's the breaths you take, that is a glorious thing to thank God for. I have met lots of people with some pretty tragic, painful stories, but even they can find some aspect of their life that isn't clouded by suffering. I challenge you too to look around, hard if you must, for *something* to thank God for today.

A simple habit you can start is to write down three things you are thankful for every day. If you practice the habit of gratitude, then your attitude and behavior will follow. God will use your heart of thanksgiving to heal and redeem you. Soon you will easily recognize the good in a bad situation.

So who am I? And who are you? It is a beautifully helpful exercise to take note of all the things you as a believer in Christ are said to be throughout Scripture. Here are just a few (adapted from The Grace Walk Experience, by Steve McVey):

A saint

"to all who are beloved of God in Rome, called as saints: Grace to you and peace from God our Father and the Lord Jesus Christ."
Romans 1:7

"To the church of God which is at Corinth, to those who have been sanctified in Christ Jesus, saints by calling, with all who in every place call on the name of our Lord Jesus Christ, their Lord and ours"
1 Corinthians 1:2

God's work of art

"For we are His workmanship, created in Christ Jesus for good works, which God prepared beforehand so that we would walk in them."
Ephesians 2:10

Righteous

"For if by the transgression of the one, death reigned through the one, much more those who receive the abundance of grace and of the gift of righteousness will reign in life through the One, Jesus Christ."
Romans 5:17

"He made Him who knew no sin to be sin on our behalf, so that we might become the righteousness of God in Him."
2 Corinthians 5:21

Chosen, holy, and blameless

"[3]Blessed be the God and Father of our Lord Jesus Christ, who has blessed us with every spiritual blessing in the heavenly places in Christ, [4]just as He chose us in Him before the foundation of the world, that we would be holy and blameless before Him."
Ephesians 1:3-4

Child of God, beloved

"In love [5]He predestined us to adoption as sons through Jesus Christ to Himself, according to the kind intention of His will, [6]to the praise of the glory of His grace, which He freely bestowed on us in the Beloved."
Ephesians 1:5-6

Redeemed, forgiven

"In Him we have redemption through His blood, the forgiveness of our trespasses, according to the riches of His grace"
Ephesians 1:7

In Christ, you are righteous, sanctified, and redeemed

"[30]But by His doing you are in Christ Jesus, who became to us wisdom from God, and righteousness and sanctification, and redemption, [31]so that, just as it is written, 'Let him who boasts, boast in the Lord.'"
1 Corinthians 1:30-31

Your identity is in Christ. This identity was given to you the moment you trusted in Christ for eternal salvation, and it can *never* be taken away from you. This identity is paramount to all other identities you may have defined yourself by in the past. Your identity in Christ is independent of your behavior, actions, roles, ethnicity, and circumstances in life. No matter what you do, no matter what happens to you, you will always be fully loved, accepted, and redeemed by God through Christ. You are His beloved child, so precious to Him that He sacrificed His Son for you just so that He could welcome you into His family for all eternity. When you experience suffering and begin to question your identity, reflect back on these truths in Scripture to remember who you really are.

"Therefore if anyone is in Christ, he is a new creature; the old things passed away; behold, new things have come."
2 Corinthians 5:17

CHAPTER 7
The Muscle of Faith

A couple of years ago, I set a lofty goal for myself: I wanted to be able to do ten pull-ups without assistance – no kipping, swinging, jumping, or using bands. Some of you reading this may easily be capable of doing that, but for me, I was hardly able to do one pull-up without assistance, and I still had to kind of jump a little to have some momentum to get out of the dead-hang.

One workout program that Michael and I like to use is so wonderful because the creator is a physical therapist, so healthy form is a big concern of his. He has also created a great program with lots of variety, which is my favorite thing when it comes to working out. I cannot stand the type of workout programs where you buy a DVD set and watch the same people, saying the same cheesy lines over and over, week after week. Boredom is a de-motivator for me. The program we use isn't a walkthrough type where you're doing the workout along with the instructor. Instead, he will demonstrate each move, but then it's your responsibility to go do the workout for that day.

One of the month-long programs focuses on pull-ups. It creates a daily workout regimen based on how many pull-ups you're able to perform when you start the month, even if it's barely one like me. In addition to working out other parts of the body, it has you perform pull-ups in between sets. At the end of that month, I was able to perform six pull-ups! Wanting to get to ten, I decided to just repeat that program for another month, this time starting at six pull-ups.

And you guys...I did it! I even have video proof! I was actually able to squeak out ten pull-ups without assistance!

Not everything can be achieved by just working hard enough, but I was so glad to reach this goal. All the days of hard work and commitment had paid off in helping me to achieve a goal I set for myself. That was a great feeling of accomplishment.

Faith, or trusting God, is like a muscle in many ways. When trying to build muscle, you can attempt a wide variety of approaches, but the reality is it takes consistency and time to build. There are no quick fixes. It cannot be rushed and cannot be shortcut. It requires endurance and a conscious choice to focus on it.

And like working out your muscles, faith can be a painful process at times. You may not know this if you're not interested in fitness, but in order to build muscle, your existing muscle fibers must first break down, then rebuild stronger than before. The suffering that I've experienced has certainly felt like it was breaking me down! The weights you lift are usually pretty heavy, much like the circumstances in your life that require faith to endure well. Soreness can linger for a time afterward as well.

But as you build muscle, your body adapts and is able to perform the same exercise more easily and efficiently, like muscle memory. That's why a variety of exercise and increasing weights results in the best fitness, as opposed to doing the same tasks at the same weight amounts.

Much like muscle memory, you can practice having faith or trusting God with the circumstances in your life. The more you practice, the easier it gets over time for that to be one of your first reactions to a situation. I'm certainly not an expert at this; I feel like I will always be learning how to better trust God with more and more of my life. But I love the idea that, like muscle building, you can begin to see progress of growth even if you're still growing.

❧

September 2014 was not a good month. Early in the month we came home from Bible study to find young Maddi kitten hanging by one of her back legs from the front-loading washing machine (we would always leave the door open when not in use so it wouldn't mildew). She must have tried to jump from the covered litter box up onto the washing machine but slipped, and her back leg just happened to get wedged in the crevice of the circular door near the hinge.

It was a horrific and traumatizing scene to walk into. Our dogs were freaking out, Maddi was frantically yowling in pain, and there was some blood on the wall. Michael rushed over to Maddi to try to hold her to take the weight off her leg. But of course a cat in distress does not want to be held, and so she bit his hands several times.

With adrenaline surging through our bodies, we tried to act quickly. The Lord must have put it on my mind to tell Michael to grab the back of Maddi's neck (like a mother carries her kittens) so that he could hold her up but not be bitten. I put the dogs outside to get them out of the way. I remembered that I still had some of Fred's leftover syringes of oral pain medicine, so I quickly shot a dose of that down Maddi's throat to hopefully relieve some of her agony.

Then we tried to figure out how to free her leg from the door crevice. The washing machine was next to a wall, so we couldn't open the door past 90-degrees. I tried removing the door but couldn't access the screws because I needed the door to open wider than 90-degrees. After about 15 minutes of this no-win situation, I had no idea what to do. I remember calling my mom in a panic (they live about 10 minutes away), and thankfully her hearing the words, "MADDI...LEG...STUCK..." was enough for her to hang up to head over. I wanted to call 911 for help but then realized that the police are far too busy to care about helping save a kitten's leg. We had to get her to a vet ASAP, but we needed her leg free to do that. So I gritted my teeth, shoved my fingers underneath Maddi's leg in the crevice, and forced it up and out. As someone who is very squeamish and cannot stand blood and gore, Michael (and I) was shocked that I could do something like that. I credit the adrenaline because it was not a pleasant thing to do, but it had to be done.

With Maddi finally free, we quickly called my parents to have them meet us at the vet instead of our house and drove Maddi to the vet school in our city (one perk of living in a city with a university). I may or may not have exceeded the speed limit by 25 mph and ran several red lights…

Once we got her checked in to the emergency care at the vet school, I then broke down in tears with the stress and trauma of it all. We had just adopted this little kitten, and now she's broken! We thought they may have to amputate the leg, but by God's grace, she was an excellent candidate for surgery. They used a plate and screws to rejoin the bones. After eight weeks of having to be confined to a kennel, she is now completely healed (although a little crazy at times). And in case you're wondering, since that day and for as long as I live with an indoor cat, I have kept a rolled up towel shoved in the crevice of our washing machine door when it's left open to dry.

Later in the month of September, we received some very tragic news. Michael's mom, Lisa, was diagnosed with metastatic breast cancer and told she had a few months left to live. Having battled cancer twice already (and going through chemotherapy treatments both times), she decided she did not want to go through that horror again. It was heartbreaking news.

We had hope at first that maybe the doctor was wrong. Maybe she would overcome this. But in early November her pain worsened. The metastases had spread to her bones already, and the pain was getting much worse for her. It became clear that she would not survive this. Michael had the beautiful idea to interview his mom on video camera to get her life story. It was nothing professional by any means, just them sitting on the couch in her apartment and talking about her life while I filmed it. I'm so glad we did that.

❧

A couple of weeks later – two days before my birthday – a friend I've known since elementary school had been in town visiting her parents for a couple weeks and knew that we were hoping to adopt. Since she couldn't fly back with it, she offered to give us all the extra breast milk that she had pumped while she was in town. Not knowing how long we would have to wait to receive a baby, but knowing breast milk can stay frozen for about a year, we gratefully accepted this generous gift and picked up a large cooler of milk from her that day. We hoped that we might get to use this "liquid gold" for our adopted newborn before it expired.

Then the day after my 30th birthday, while at work, I received a phone call on my cell phone from the same area code as our adoption agency. It was in fact our caseworker. She wished me a belated happy birthday and said she had a wonderful present to give me. She said, "A birth mother has chosen you guys to adopt her baby." Not wanting Michael to miss out, I asked her to please hold, dialed Michael's number on my work phone, and told him to come down to my office immediately (he worked two floors up from my office). Once he arrived I asked our caseworker to repeat what she said.

She told us that a birth mother saw our online profile and fell in love with us. She didn't want to see any other parent profiles; she was sure of her decision. She was pregnant with a baby girl and was due one month later. She considered herself a diehard vegetarian and loved that we are passionate about eating a plant-based diet. The very thing that we were nervous about putting in our profile was the thing that first stood out to her! I began to weep with the beauty of God's sweet gift to us. Sometimes the very thing that you feel insecure about is the very thing that God will use to show His glory and grace.

To say that the next month was chaotic is an understatement. Lisa's pain worsened to the point that she saw

97

specialists at MD Anderson to receive radiation treatments, not in the hopes of treating her cancer, but simply to relieve some of her bone pain. She also had masses in her lungs, brain, and liver. Her condition quickly declined, and she reached a point where she was unable to live alone. She was admitted to the hospital for a few weeks.

During this time, my sweet and loving friends and co-workers really showered us with God's love. They threw together a massive baby shower with just two weeks notice. Having expected to wait for about 15 months for a baby, we had nothing yet. Not a single baby item. But by the time our daughter was born, we had all the basics and much more. I was so humbled and touched by how God provided so much for us through our loved ones.

In early December, we met the birth family for the first time. We were a little nervous, but it was also incredibly beautiful. We met at a vegetarian restaurant in their city, which was fun to try. The neat thing about our particular adoption match situation was that both the birth mother and father and their families were involved and supportive of the birth mother's decision to place this baby for adoption. It is very common for adoptive parents to only have contact with the birth mother and maybe her parents.

We learned more about the birth family and why they chose us. The birth father's side had a love of animals and gardening, something that Michael is very passionate about. We learned about the birth parents' interests and shared laughs and stories as we got to know one another. We took silly pictures together too, which are fun to look back at.

At one point the birth mother and her mom asked us what we were planning to name the baby. We told them, "Elizabeth." They looked at one another and said, "That's the name we were talking about." Chills!

The neatest part about that first meeting was witnessing how incredible this birth mother and father were handling their situation. They were both young and in high school, hoping to attend college afterward. Yet even in their youth, they had the maturity, love, and wisdom to choose to keep this child alive and make a loving plan for their baby.

I remember feeling some fears and insecurities when we first applied to our adoption agency: "What if the birth family wants the baby back one day?" "What if our adopted child hates us and wants to go live with their birth family instead?" What if this and what if that. But in the moment that we received that phone call from our caseworker telling us that a birth mother had chosen us – us, out of all the other potential adoptive parents out there – we felt such a strong feeling of love for the birth family.

After we first met the birth family, we felt such excitement because we felt like while our biological family was getting smaller, our family was really getting bigger because God was joining our family with this birth family. I was so thankful and amazed at how our loving God had planned all of this out.

As Lisa continued to suffer in the hospital, she asked us to please get rid of all her stuff and her apartment. We adopted her dog, bringing our pet headcount to six: three dogs and three cats. We sold a lot of her stuff and found someone to take over her apartment lease. It was so overwhelming to handle all of this plus prepare to become parents in a short amount of time.

I remember breaking down one night in the car with Michael. I was upset because I had been dreaming of the moment for years when Michael and I would be preparing for a baby together, and I felt like this precious remaining time of "just us" was being robbed from us by having to handle everything for Lisa. And then I felt so guilty for thinking something so selfish. His mom was so sweet, and she was dying. She had no control over the timing of when she would die, but there I was, upset because of how all of this was negatively impacting me. I'm glad I expressed those honest feelings, but I'm also thankful for God's grace to forgive my incessant selfishness and struggles with control. It was yet another thing I had to accept, surrender, and trust God with.

We visited Lisa often in the hospital and tried to help her

feel included in our adoption by showing her pictures of the birth family and talk to her about all the baby gifts we had received.

The birth family invited us to be present at the hospital for the birth. The birth mother went a couple days past her due date and was induced on a Friday. Lisa's situation and Elizabeth's birth were colliding in time. As we drove the couple of hours away to attend her birth, Lisa was transferred from the hospital to a facility to care for her until she passed away.

Once we arrived at the hospital, the birth family invited us into the labor room, where the birth mother was hooked up to a fetal heart rate monitor. The first sound I heard as we entered that room was Elizabeth's heart beat, the most incredible sound I'd ever heard.

We enjoyed talking with the birth family for an hour or so but also didn't want to overstay our welcome. We excused ourselves to go eat lunch in the cafeteria. Several hours later, I received a text message from the birth grandmother (birth mother's mom) saying that her daughter was about to start pushing, and everyone else had been asked to leave to wait in the waiting room. We joined the family in the waiting room and enjoyed getting to know them even more.

A little after 4:00 PM, I received a phone call from the birth grandmother. But when I answered all I heard was a baby crying...my daughter's first cry! So that you can understand how sweet this gift was, allow me to explain how the adoption law is in Texas. In Texas, when parents want to place their baby for adoption, they cannot legally sign the parental relinquishment papers until the baby is 48-hours-old or older. Any interaction the adoptive parents have with the baby and the birth family prior to this form being signed is nothing short of a gift. They do not have to include adoptive parents in the birth at all. But they wanted us there, and she wanted me to hear Elizabeth's first cry as she entered this world.

They also wanted Michael and me to come hold Elizabeth during her first hour of life. Again, this was such a sweet and generous gift. When we walked in the room and saw our daughter for the first time, we were overjoyed. I do, however, remember thinking as they handed Elizabeth to me, "She's beautiful!" followed immediately by, "Oh my Lord, I have NO idea how to take care of her!" Remember, I'm an only child, I didn't babysit much, and because of our infertility, I intentionally did not read any baby care books. Then with only a month's notice and all the stuff we were handling regarding Lisa's illness, we didn't have time to read anything to prepare for a baby. I was really impressed and grateful when Michael took the lead on learning how to feed and change her from the nurses.

Bitter and sweet had never been so intermixed in our lives before. Lisa was barely able to speak by this point, so when Michael called her to tell her that Elizabeth had been born, it was mostly a one-way conversation. I remember Michael breaking down in the lobby because he was sad that he was losing the ability to hear her voice and that she wasn't there in person to share in the moment.

My parents drove up the next day and got to meet Elizabeth while she was in the hospital nursery. Michael and I tried to enjoy our last weekend of just the two of us. Even though we were sad that Lisa was missing out on this experience, we were also happy to have met our daughter.

That Sunday night, after the birth parents signed the relinquishment papers, we drove home as a family of three. After four years of waiting, we were finally parents!

We took Elizabeth to the care facility to meet Lisa. Lisa was no longer able to speak, but she smiled and looked the happiest we had seen her in many weeks as she gazed at and touched her newest granddaughter.

Knowing that Lisa's passing was imminent, I told Michael that he should focus on spending time with his mom, and I would handle all of the newborn care. Michael read the Bible to Lisa, prayed with her, and told her how much he loved her. We knew she trusted in Christ, so we knew she would go to heaven. I remember praying for the Lord to take her, to end her suffering. We were all ready and yet so not ready.

Lisa passed away eight days after Elizabeth was born. We were thankful that God allowed Lisa to meet Elizabeth before she died. We were also glad that she was no longer in pain and was rejoicing in heaven with Jesus.

It was difficult to process all of the things that she would miss because she was no longer with us on earth – getting to watch Elizabeth grow up, be a Grammy to her, and see Michael as a father. But as Michael regularly said (as much to himself as to me): it's best to focus on what we've gained, not on what we've lost. Those were very wise words that the Lord placed on his heart.

❧

All we had to rely on during that overwhelming month was our faith. We had faith that God would make us parents if that was His will. We had faith in the body of Christ to help us when we were in need. We had faith in God's Goodness even during that time of mourning. We believe that Lisa entered heaven because of her faith in Christ.

Hebrews 11:1 says "Now faith is the assurance of things hoped for, the conviction of things not seen."

When you look at the Greek word for "assurance" it is "hupostasis," which means "that which has foundation, is firm; the steadfastness of mind, firmness, courage, resolution; confidence, firm trust, assurance." Isn't that beautiful imagery? When you feel the world crumbling around you because of the suffering you're experiencing, your faith in Christ is your firm foundation as well as the steadfastness of your mind.

Furthermore, Hebrews 1:1-3 describes Jesus, and in verse 3 in particular, the Greek word "hupostasis" is used again but in a very affirmative way. It says, "And He is the radiance of His glory and the exact representation of His *nature*, and upholds all things by the word of His power. When He had made purification of sins, He sat down at the right hand of the Majesty on high."

Jesus' nature is "hupostasis," or in other words, His very nature is a firm foundation. How marvelous is that!? Christ, who is in you, is your firm foundation. He is *always* with you, so rest assured that no matter what storms come you *always* have a firm foundation to stand on.

❦

2015 began as a flurry of new parenting experiences. We had waited so long to become parents, so I think that helped us to keep a bigger perspective about the work involved in raising a baby. Maternal instincts I didn't know I had took shape and soon enough I felt like an expert at feeding, changing, and sleep scheduling our sweet baby girl.

It was a sweet answer to prayer and an incredible joy to see Elizabeth's first smile, hear her first laugh, cheer when she first crawled, and ~~panic at the sudden change to our routine~~ rejoice when she took her first steps before ten months old. She was and is an intelligent and eager child. She is always trying to figure things out and wanting to participate in what we're doing.

But they say "death comes in threes." This is of course not a law of the universe, and we are not superstitious people in the least, but this cliché happened to be true for us.

At the beginning of 2015, my sweet 94-year-old Meemaw was diagnosed with peritoneal cancer (the layer of tissue that lies inside the abdomen). My Meemaw was an incredible grandmother to me. She lived in the same city since I was four years old, and I would regularly spend the night at her house. She indulged my silly imagination to run around her living room on hands and knees, pretending to be *all* the horses at a horse show, where I would jump over her snack trays that I turned on their sides. She may or may not have obliged my request to cut up apple slices and let me eat them out of her hand like a horse would have...

She was a caring and servant-hearted woman who was very active in her church. She was also a very tough old lady, so it was hard to see her suffering in pain from her cancer. She was the type who would not readily admit she was in pain unless it was *really* bad, so we knew it was serious when she said her stomach hurt.

Her mental acuity had been declining for several years but was at its worst during her last few months. They say it's common for short-term memory to go first, so she never forgot who I was, but I remember visiting her near the end of her life. When she first saw me, she had a surprised expression on her face as she said, "Christine! You're so beautiful!" She was speaking as if she could only remember me as a child, like she was seeing me as an adult for the first time.

She passed away in April. She was a month shy of turning 95 years old. Again, I was grateful to know that she had trusted in Christ and that she is now rejoicing with Him in heaven, but I still miss her presence here on earth.

The third loss took place less than a month after Meemaw passed away. David, the man who first shared the gospel with Michael in high school and had discipled him, had been diagnosed with brain cancer and died in early May 2015. Although we hadn't seen him or Sue in person for many years, we kept in touch via email.

We had always felt so grateful that God led them to our city for the short time they were there. Even though the reason they moved to our city (to work at a church) fell through, which was really difficult for them, we felt like God brought them to our city just for us. I know that isn't true, but that's how we always felt. It was just such an odd circumstance that they packed up and moved their whole family to our city, specifically to work at a church, but when it fell through, they decided to make the best of the situation and go door-to-door to share the Good News of the Gospel. If it wasn't for their suffering that unexpected situation and their faithfulness to the Lord to make the best of a bad situation, Michael may never have accepted Christ, and we likely would not have ended up together.

Even their story of experiencing suffering with unmet

expectations regarding a job and relocation is a neat example of how much good God brought out of that suffering. Sometimes we just cannot see the bigger picture of God's plan working through our hardships.

❦

Wherever you are in the process of struggling with something, you can decide to begin working out your muscle of faith. You can decide to trust God with your circumstances and know that He is good, and He is working your situation out for good, even if you don't understand or see how yet. There is hope in the growth that's taking place in your heart.

CHAPTER 8

Work Together for Good

I have always thought pearls are beautiful. I borrowed my Granny's pearl necklace for my wedding day and felt that it added a level of classiness to my gown. Natural pearls are formed in the soft tissue of mollusks in response to an injury or a parasite. Like the human body's immune system that forms a scab on a wound, the mollusk's system forms a pearl sac that over time grows and hardens into a pearl.

The most valuable pearls are natural pearls, but most of the pearls in the jewelry industry are cultured (farmed) pearls because natural pearls are too rare to keep up with the demand. Imitation pearls can look decent but lack the inherent smoothness, sheen, and beauty of natural or cultured pearls.

It's amazing to me how a traumatic event in the mollusk's life can result in something so rare and beautiful. This process reminds me of the hope we have in Christ: suffering leads to something rare, extremely valuable, and beautiful beyond belief. And like imitation pearls, there is no shortcutting the process. You don't get the pearl without enduring the pain, refinement, and time that leads to it.

God is always at work in your life. He sees every painful situation, every loss, every heartache, and every tear you shed. He is actively refining your character and healing your heart. If you keep trusting Him, He will form your suffering into a pearl.

A Biblical example of this is the story of Joseph in Genesis 37-50. I encourage you to take the time to read all of it on your own, but I'll summarize the events here.

Joseph had a bit of a dysfunctional family. His father was Jacob, who was tricked into marrying Leah and then finally married Rachel, whom he loved the most. Between his two wives and each wife's maid he had 12 sons. But like he had a favorite wife, he also had a favorite son, Joseph, the firstborn of his favorite wife. As is typical in a favoritism situation, it doesn't go over very well with the non-favorites.

Several of the other brothers disliked Joseph and plotted to kill him. Reuben, the oldest son, suggested not to kill him but to throw him in a pit instead. He planned to sneak back to the pit later and take Joseph back home. A different brother, Judah, out of selfishness, suggested selling Joseph to the group of people traveling to Egypt. And so they did. The other brothers told their father, Jacob, that Joseph had been killed by a wild animal.

But God was looking out for all of them. Joseph prospered in Egypt, rising up the ranks to become second only to Pharaoh because God gave Joseph the gift of interpreting dreams. Joseph was put in charge of Pharaoh's house and all the land and prepared for widespread famine that would last for seven years. Joseph gathered reserves of food that would sustain all the people during the years of famine.

When the famine came to fruition, Jacob sent all of his remaining sons – except Benjamin, his new favorite son now that he believed he had lost Joseph – to Egypt to purchase food so they wouldn't starve. Since Joseph was in charge of the food reserves, he saw his brothers approaching from a distance and decided to have some fun. Before the brothers saw Joseph, Joseph ordered that they be imprisoned. Joseph then overheard the brothers talking to one another about how they did a terrible thing selling Joseph and plotting to kill him, and they expressed remorse for it.

Joseph was moved by that and ordered that they be given the grain they came to purchase but to surreptitiously put their money back in their bags so they ended up getting the grain for free. Joseph came up with a plan to reveal his true identity to the brothers but wanted all of the brothers to be present. He ordered that all of the brothers except one be released to take the grain back home and to return with Benjamin. If they returned with Benjamin, then the final brother would be released from prison.

When the released brothers brought the grain home, they told Jacob what had happened and that they needed to return to Egypt with Benjamin. Jacob was terrified of losing another son and didn't want to send Benjamin. But Reuben, the oldest son, vowed to bring all the sons back and gave his own two sons as collateral if he failed. Judah (lineage of Christ) also promised to return all the brothers and be held personally responsible if he did not. Finally Jacob surrendered and trusted God and told them to take Benjamin, fine goods to give as a gift, and double the money (since the first grain purchase money was returned to them). Jacob even said, "And as for me, if I am bereaved of my children, I am bereaved." This is a great example of what it looks like practically to surrender. He fought to keep control for a while but finally trusted God with whatever the outcome, even the loss of his children.

When all the brothers returned to Egypt, Joseph tricked them again by sneaking his cup into Benjamin's bag. Joseph ordered that whoever had the cup in his bag would remain there and be his slave. When the cup was found in Benjamin's bag, Judah pleaded to take Benjamin's place and be Joseph's slave instead. Joseph broke down and wept with his brothers, revealing his true identity.

He said to them:

*"I am your brother Joseph, whom you sold into Egypt. Now do not be grieved or angry with yourselves, because you sold me here, for God sent me before you to preserve life. For the famine has been in the land these two years, and there are still five years in which there will be neither plowing nor harvesting. God sent me before you to preserve for you a remnant in the earth, and to keep you alive by a great deliverance. **Now, therefore,***

it was not you who sent me here, but God; and He has made me a father to Pharaoh and lord of all his household and ruler over all the land of Egypt."
Genesis 45:4-8

After the heartfelt revealing of his true identity, Joseph invited the brothers to go back home and bring Jacob and all their family to move to Egypt to live. And so they did. Jacob and everyone moved to and thrived in Egypt.

After Jacob died at an old age, Joseph's brothers became fearful.

When Joseph's brothers saw that their father was dead, they said, "What if Joseph bears a grudge against us and pays us back in full for all the wrong which we did to him!" So they sent a message to Joseph, saying, "Your father charged before he died, saying, 'Thus you shall say to Joseph, "Please forgive, I beg you, the transgression of your brothers and their sin, for they did you wrong."' And now, please forgive the transgression of the servants of the God of your father." And Joseph wept when they spoke to him. Then his brothers also came and fell down before him and said, "Behold, we are your servants." But Joseph said to them, "Do not be afraid, for am I in God's place? **As for you, you meant evil against me, but God meant it for good in order to bring about this present result, to preserve many people alive.** *So therefore, do not be afraid; I will provide for you and your little ones." So he comforted them and spoke kindly to them.*
Genesis 50:15-21

Had Reuben and Judah not suggested those alternatives to killing Joseph all those years ago, then Jacob and Joseph's brothers and lots of other people would likely have starved to death. But God had a plan for their survival the entire time. He worked good into a very bad situation.

One thing I want to point out here is that the "good" that God worked out in this situation was not known until later in their lives. It can often be true for us that we don't fully understand what God is doing behind the scenes to work good in a situation until much later in hindsight. When you're in the depths of your suffering, it can feel unfair and hopeless. But God can redeem and work good into any situation.

❦

In late July 2015, Michael and I attended a normal Sunday morning sermon at our church, but this sermon turned out to be anything but normal in our lives. The sermon was about pornography, and unlike previous sermons on the subject, the pastor also included a short segment about the impact this struggle can have on the wife. Specifically, he talked about how studies show that the negative impact on the wife is strikingly similar to symptoms of post traumatic stress disorder.

God used this sermon to convict Michael's heart about this topic. On the drive home from church, he asked me if I experienced PTSD-like symptoms. I told him that I definitely do, such as, whenever we would have a fight and he would leave the room for a while with his phone, I felt anxious and worried if he was viewing pornography.

That day was a major turning point for our marriage. Michael said he wanted to begin meeting regularly with someone for accountability and that he wanted to no longer keep this habit in the dark. We had some very open conversations in the days that followed, which started to show me that he was genuine in his decision to experience healing. It also encouraged me to begin building trust again.

Michael began to meet every other week with Pat, an older friend and pastor at our church. I cannot speak enough about how impactful this relationship has been for Michael's life and our marriage. Unlike all previous attempts Michael made to seek accountability (where he felt there was hypocrisy and a lack of vulnerability and grace), Pat took a very different approach: grace. He suggested that they discuss the workbook for a book called The Grace Walk by Steve McVey. While The Grace Walk book itself is very good, the workbook (titled The Grace Walk Experience) is a wonderful guide to understanding

111

God's grace in a very personal way.

When Michael began to share some of the concepts that the workbook discusses about grace, I became intrigued to read through it myself. That workbook revealed so many misconceptions I had been holding onto for most of my Christian life.

I formerly had the view of God as a Father whose favor would fluctuate based on my performance. In other words, if I was consistent in my behavior with reading the Bible, attending church, and being a "good Christian," then God was pleased with me. But when I fell out of those spiritual habits and experienced a spiritual slump, then God was disappointed in me. This led me to struggle with so much guilt and shame over my walk with the Lord.

But The Grace Walk Experience helped me understand that from the moment I accepted Christ, I became a new creation. I had read this verse many times before, but for the first time, it really got through to me. It helped me understand that while we are all born as sinners, when you accept Christ, you become a saint. As a believer, you are no longer a sinner because Christ conquered sin once and for all. Instead, you are a saint who sometimes sins. But sin is no longer your master. This means that when God looks at you, He only sees Christ. So God's view of you does not change based on your behavior – He only sees Christ. God is always delighted with you and loves you because He delights in and loves Christ. He doesn't delight in the sinful behavior, but He adores and delights in you, His precious child.

Ever since I finished reading that book, Scripture has come alive to me in ways it never had before. One of my new favorite verses that summarizes my new understanding is 1 Corinthians 1:30-31:

"[30]But by His doing you are in Christ Jesus, who became to us wisdom from God, and righteousness and sanctification, and redemption, [31]so that, just as it is written, 'Let him who boasts, boast in the Lord.'"
1 Corinthians 1:30-31

By His doing, Christ is our wisdom from God, our righteousness, our sanctification, and our redemption. Christ is our very source of life. We, in our fleshly bodies, still sometimes choose independence and choose to sin. But when we remember our true identity – that we are one with Christ – then we can live in dependence on Christ and experience victory over sin.

The Grace Walk Experience likewise impacted Michael in incredible ways. He finally understood that God wasn't extending guilt and shame toward him when he chose to sin sexually. He also realized that he had been trying to overcome this sinful habit for all these years by his own self-efforts, and so no wonder he always fell short. This book helped him realize that he needs to depend completely on Christ to overcome sin. It was Christ who conquered sin after all, not Michael. This allowed Michael to feel free of the self-imposed burden to beat this sin on his own. He isn't alone, ever. Depending on Christ to resist temptation on his behalf allowed Michael to experience freedom from shame and guilt and experience much longer time periods of victory over this sin.

From my perspective, Michael became a changed man, all because of Christ working through him. There had always been this elephant in the room (especially the bedroom) that was preventing us from experiencing a deeper level of intimacy in our marriage. Now that Michael was getting regular accountability and depending on Christ on a daily basis, this had a profound and wonderful impact on our marriage. We've both experienced so much healing because of God revealing His true nature to us through His Word, wise counsel, and that workbook. I'm so grateful for those transformations!

❧

In the spring of 2016, we attended an annual health festival that has become tradition for us. At this festival, there was one speaker who discussed women's hormone health and issues in relation to a plant-based diet. She was a doctor in the Austin area, and since I was still experiencing some painful periods, I thought it would be easy enough for me to see her as a patient to see if she could help me experience any relief from those symptoms naturally.

To my surprise, she connected the dots on several odd and seemingly unrelated symptoms and diagnosed me with hypothyroidism (something that I never should have developed while eating a plant-based diet) and something I had never heard of before: upper airway respiratory syndrome.

A CT scan of my sinuses/airway and a sleep study confirmed that diagnosis. She explained that essentially I wasn't getting very restful sleep because my sleep study revealed that I woke up slightly every 20 minutes. (And I had always thought it was normal to wake up half a dozen times at night or more!) My oxygen level would start at 100% then dip to about 92%, which would then cause me to wake up just enough to take a deep breath to reset my oxygen level to 100% and so on. I was a mouth-breather and had been my whole life. And the CT scan showed that I had a deviated septum and my throat airway was very narrow because my maxilla didn't grow forward properly as a child.

All of these issues combined resulted in me not breathing well, especially when trying to sleep at night. My doctor explained that over years and years of not getting good sleep, parasympathetic systems that aren't critical for survival, such as the digestive, immune, and reproductive systems, don't get the proper attention they need in the deeper stages of sleep because I was never reaching the deeper stages of sleep. That could explain why I developed an autoimmune hypothyroidism condition and perhaps why my hormones were still not optimal. She recommended that I get sinus surgery as a first step to allow me to breathe through my nose as best as possible.

Michael became curious about himself and went through the same diagnostic process, and it turned out that he was waking up every 10 minutes – often enough that he was diagnosed with sleep apnea.

We both had sinus surgery in September 2016, one week apart from one another because why not be miserable together? In all seriousness, I'm so glad we got that surgery (and we do not agree to surgery lightly!) because after healing, we started breathing through our noses at night and started getting much better sleep.

A few months before our sinus surgeries, we began to notice some odd symptoms from our German Shepherd, Abby. She would lightly drag her back foot when she walked, and it slowly wore down her nails until the quicks (the flesh beneath the nail) bled.

After a basic Google search, Michael discovered an unfortunately common disease to German Shepherds that we had never heard of, despite doing research on the breed before we got her as a puppy eight years prior. The disease is called degenerative myelopathy, and it's a chronic, incurable disease that slowly results in the dog losing its ability to control its hind end.

We didn't want to assume the worst without additional confirmation from a vet, so we began the process of seeing a canine specialist (again, another blessing of living in a city with a vet school) to eliminate potential other causes. We also submitted Abby's DNA sample to a national organization that can detect whether the dog has one or two abnormal copies of the degenerative myelopathy gene.

Sadly, Abby had two abnormal copies and the specialist eliminated all other causes, so we had to accept the reality that our sweet Shepherd would slowly decline until she reached a point where we had to decide enough was enough to put her down. The weird thing about this disease (but also a blessing) is that the dog doesn't feel pain as they lose bodily control. It's typical for the dog's owner to make the decision to euthanize when the situation reaches a point of too much stress from having to clean up after the dog going potty inside or having to physically help the dog move around to get enough food and water.

We hated having the power to decide when to end her life. I suppose all pet owners have this power, but for me, this felt unlike any previous experience I'd had with pets. In the past, it had always been undoubtedly clear when it was "time" to put the pet to sleep. But this time would be very different.

In the months that followed, we tried to stay positive and enjoy the time we had left with Abby. I took a ton of pictures and videos so that I could remember as much as possible after she passed: her laying on the floor giving me those puppy eyes, her playing keep away from the other dogs, the sound of her barking in the backyard.

Having discovered her disease in the summer, we didn't know how quickly she would decline. In my head, I didn't think she would live past my birthday in November, but she did. She had to wear protective boots on her back feet to avoid bleeding quicks, and she had already lost control over her bowels, releasing them wherever she happened to be standing. But she could still walk and sometimes run. She was able to join us for our annual Christmas trip to a cabin with family.

But shortly after Christmas, she then lost control of her bladder too. Her condition was definitely starting to negatively impact our marriage and stress levels. Every morning we would exit the bedroom with anxiety, worrying if she had pooped inside and then stepped in it, smooshing it into the carpet. Cleaning up that mess became a daily occurrence, on top of our other household, pet, and parenting responsibilities.

Just before New Year's Eve, we both agreed to put her to sleep in about one week. It was heartbreaking to schedule a euthanasia. And I'm pretty sure I cried every single day during her last week as I tried not to think about the impending doom that was coming closer each day, but it was of course impossible for me to forget. But we knew that she was not going to get better, only worse, because that's the nature of that disease.

On January 4th, 2017, Michael took the afternoon off from

work. We planned to take Abby to the vet at 1:00PM to have her put down. Before we loaded her into our car, we wanted to have one last happy moment with her. We threw her favorite Kong toy in the front yard so she could play with and fetch it.

Then we all drove to the vet together. The nice receptionist agreed to let Elizabeth play behind her desk while Michael and I went into the room with Abby. We both were sobbing the whole time. I just squatted down in front of Abby's sweet face and petted her the whole time, telling her how much I love her and how good of a girl she is. I wanted her last image in this world to be one of love.

I have no idea if it's Biblical or true, but I really, really hope that pets end up in heaven even though they do not have souls like human beings. I know God loves animals because He created them. I just hope He allows our beloved animals to be there too.

❧

When facing the loss of someone you love dearly, it can be impossible to imagine how God can work something for good out of something so painful. Our society especially wonders what good could possibly come out of something as awful as the death of a child. Most people can wrap their mind around the unexpected death of an adult, but when it's a child – particularly a baby – it can really challenge a person in their faith in God and His Goodness. How can that horrible situation possibly result in any good? Sometimes the answer is obvious and sometimes it's more mysterious, but trust that He is working for good whether you notice it or not.

Although society may disagree, to God, every person is precious, and His heart aches when any of His children are harmed. Yet He willingly gave His Son over to those who would crucify Him. How could God allow such a thing? How could God sit by and watch as Jesus was severely beaten, ridiculed, forced to carry His own torment device, nailed to it, had a crown of thorns shoved into the flesh of His scalp, hoisted upright on the cross so that for each and every breath He had to excruciatingly lift His bodyweight up, and finally collapsed in death?

"For the wages of sin is death, but the free gift of God is eternal life in Christ Jesus our Lord."
Romans 6:23

The penalty for sin had to be death. And because God wanted to make a way for all of mankind to be able to spend eternity with Him in heaven, He sent His perfect, sinless substitute to take the penalty of death that we deserved to suffer. The Pharisees intended evil for Jesus, but God intended Good. Out of love, He sacrificed the Most Precious One for us.

Jesus said to him, "I am the way, and the truth, and the life; no one comes to the Father but through Me."
John 14:6

God worked Good in the worst situation in history. That is the Good News of the gospel. Because of Christ, we have the opportunity to believe in Him and gain eternal life.

My favorite verse is:

"And we know that God causes all things to work together for good to those who love God, to those who are called according to His purpose."
Romans 8:28

Good can come from any amount of suffering. Good comes in different shapes and sizes. It may be character growth, personal growth in your faith or ability to trust God, or it may simply be God receiving glory in the situation. "Good" in this verse is the Greek word "agathos," which is also used in Scripture as "kind" and "generous." When I read those words, I get the sense of a gift being given to us. Have you ever thought of your circumstances like that? The suffering you're facing may actually be a good gift being given to you for a good purpose. If good is not evident in your situation, I encourage you to make effort to seek it out. Even go so far as to make a list. God is a Good God, and a Good, Good, Father. He delights in you, cares deeply for you, and is most surely working good in your suffering somehow, someway.

CHAPTER 9
Hope Does Not Disappoint

I'm not always the biggest fan of musicals, but there are a few that I completely adore. One recent musical that I've fallen in love with is *The Greatest Showman*. In this movie starring Hugh Jackman that depicts the life of P.T. Barnum (spoiler alert), his character grew up poor but had a loving wife and two daughters. He struggled with discontentment and was always seeking more. He built a successful circus show and later partnered with Phillip Carlyle (played by Zac Efron).

As his circus show grew in popularity, he eventually brought Jenny Lind, a famous European singer, into the show that helped grow it even more. By this time, P.T. Barnum and his family owned a large luxurious home, and he traveled on tour with Jenny to continue gaining wealth and power, leaving his circus performer friends and Phillip to pick up the slack back home. He allowed his thirst for more to cloud his judgment and ended up in an intimate almost-kissed situation with Jenny because he hadn't realized her feelings for him. He declined her advances, but in a public performance, she quickly stole a kiss from him, which was photographed by reporters. He immediately left to return home to his family.

P.T. Barnum really hit a rock bottom moment when he returned home to find that his circus building had caught fire, and he had to go rescue his friend Phillip. To pour salt on the wound, he learned that Jenny quit, and her stolen kiss with him was published in the newspapers, which meant that his wife had surely found out before he'd had a chance to tell her.

When he arrived back at their home, his wife was packing up to leave, not only because she was angry about Jenny kissing her husband, but they were also being evicted from their house because he had been borrowing against their house to fund the traveling singing performances.

Dejected and alone, he wound up drinking in a bar. But he wasn't alone for long. His circus performer friends came to remind him that he's never alone, no matter how badly he messed up or hurt their feelings by prioritizing fame over their well-being. They helped remind him that he need not gain wealth and power from the world because he had been wealthy all along – rich with a loving family and everlasting friendships.

P.T. Barnum had no reason to hope. He had lost everything. But just like God is always present and promises to never leave you, his true friends were there to remind him to pursue the things that are truly worthy.

"¹Therefore, having been justified by faith, we have peace with God through our Lord Jesus Christ, ²through whom also we have obtained our introduction by faith into this grace in which we stand; and we exult in hope of the glory of God. ³And not only this, but we also exult in our tribulations, knowing that tribulation brings about perseverance; ⁴and perseverance, proven character; and proven character, hope; ⁵and hope does not disappoint, because the love of God has been poured out within our hearts through the Holy Spirit who was given to us."
Romans 5:1-5

These verses were my original inspiration to begin blogging about our infertility journey. Hope. I fought desperately to maintain hope. When I started my period, yet again. When someone said something insensitive to me. When the enemy began crowding my thoughts with despair and doubts. When my tears burned down my cheeks. I needed hope. We all need hope.

And we have it.

Notice in verse 1 where peace comes from: through Christ and because of Christ. Because our faith in Christ justifies us before God, we have access to peace from God. It is ours if we choose to trust Christ for it.

And in verse 2, it is also through Christ that we stand in grace. We are covered in grace because of Jesus. It's not about what we've done; it's about what Jesus already did. It is finished, and it is everlasting, and it is freely yours if you accept that as truth. This is why we have hope.

Verses 3-5 are where you get a hefty dose of reality. There is no prosperity gospel here. Whether you believe in Jesus or you don't, you will still suffer in this world. No one can do or be good enough to escape suffering. Jesus was perfect and suffered greatly.

When suffering or tribulations come your way, verse 3 says we are to exult in them. This word, exult, comes from the Greek word, kauchaomai, which means "to glory (whether with reason or without)." In other words, whether it makes sense yet or not, we are to remember that the purpose of suffering tribulations is to glorify God.

There is encouragement for the sufferer too: suffering leads to perseverance, which leads to proven character, which leads to hope. Another way of thinking about this is that when you experience hardships, and you continue to surrender to and trust in Christ, then you are in for an incredible journey. Let's look closer.

Tribulation brings about perseverance. Perseverance comes from the Greek word, hupomone, which is defined as:

> *steadfastness;*
> *constancy;*
> *endurance;*
> *a patient, steadfast waiting for;*
> *in the New Testament it is the characteristic of a man who is not swerved from his deliberate purpose and his loyalty to faith and piety by even the greatest trials and sufferings*

I love these definitions. These all describe God and His character too. Hebrews 13:8 says, "Jesus Christ is the same yesterday and today and forever." Perseverance is a godly trait, and if we display that trait, then that's one way God is glorified through our suffering.

Perseverance leads to proven character. "Proven character" comes from the Greek word, dokime, which means "approved, tried character; a proof, a specimen of tried worth." When I read this definition, it makes me feel so confident in my place in God's kingdom. It reminds me that I am not defined by my suffering; I'm defined by Christ. It's already done. Your worth is found in Jesus. Your identity in Christ means you don't have to wrestle with the lie of being good enough.

Lastly, proven character leads to hope. Hope here comes from the Greek word, elpis, which means:

expectation of good, hope;
in the Christian sense, joyful and confident expectation of eternal
salvation;
the author of hope, or he who is its foundation

We have hope in the promise that we have eternal salvation through Christ, and we have hope that Christ is in us. The author of hope is in us. He is our firm foundation.

And this hope does not disappoint, or "dishonor, disgrace, make us ashamed." People feel shame so easily. It's nice to be reminded that when we place our hope in Jesus, we are no longer subject to shame. We are free. We are redeemed. All because of Christ.

"For the word of the cross is foolishness to those who are perishing, but to
us who are being saved it is the power of God."
1 Corinthians 1:18

This life is all about glorifying God through our hope in Jesus Christ. Even when it makes no sense to have hope.

In 1 Samuel 17, the Israelites were facing a battle with the Philistines. The Philistines had a prized weapon: Goliath, a giant who stood over 9-feet tall. Goliath taunted the Israelites by challenging them to select one warrior to fight with him, whereby the losers would be forced into servitude of the victors. Verse 11 says, "When Saul and all Israel heard these words of the Philistine, they were dismayed and greatly afraid."

This taunting challenge continued for 40 days! During that time, David, the youngest of eight sons of Jesse, went back and forth between Bethlehem and the soldiers' camp because David's three oldest brothers were soldiers of Israel. One day David brought food for his brothers as the soldiers were marching out to the battlefield, and David overheard Goliath's taunting challenge. David then told King Saul that he would fight Goliath.

"33Then Saul said to David, 'You are not able to go against this Philistine to fight with him; for you are but a youth while he has been a warrior from his youth.' 34But David said to Saul, 'Your servant was tending his father's sheep. When a lion or a bear came and took a lamb from the flock, 35I went out after him and attacked him, and rescued it from his mouth; and when he rose up against me, I seized him by his beard and struck him and killed him. 36Your servant has killed both the lion and the bear; and this uncircumcised Philistine will be like one of them, since he has taunted the armies of the living God.' 37And David said, 'The Lord who delivered me from the paw of the lion and from the paw of the bear, He will deliver me from the hand of this Philistine.' And Saul said to David, 'Go, and may the Lord be with you.'"
1 Samuel 17:33-37

At first it seems like David was bragging about how great he was to King Saul, having defeated a lion and a bear, but then it becomes clear that David credits the Lord for fighting through him and delivering him from those enemies. He displayed great faith in the Lord to deliver him from Goliath too.

King Saul ordered David to be dressed in armor to protect him against what I'm sure he believed to be a suicide mission, but at least he would sleep better at night knowing he had done all he could to not send a youth to be squashed by a giant

Philistine. But David couldn't move with the heavy armor on, so he took it all off.

He simply collected five smooth stones and his sling, put them in his shepherd's bag, and walked out onto the battlefield toward Goliath. Goliath began to taunt David too.

"⁴⁴The Philistine also said to David, 'Come to me, and I will give your flesh to the birds of the sky and the beasts of the field.' ⁴⁵Then David said to the Philistine, 'You come to me with a sword, a spear, and a javelin, but I come to you in the name of the Lord of hosts, the God of the armies of Israel, whom you have taunted. ⁴⁶This day the Lord will deliver you up into my hands, and I will strike you down and remove your head from you. And I will give the dead bodies of the army of the Philistines this day to the birds of the sky and the wild beasts of the earth, that all the earth may know that there is a God in Israel, ⁴⁷and that all this assembly may know that the Lord does not deliver by sword or by spear; for the battle is the Lord's and He will give you into our hands.'"
1 Samuel 17:44-47

Then they charged toward one another, and David used his sling to hurl a single stone at Goliath, which hit him square in his forehead. Goliath fell and was killed. There was no logical reason to have hope that a young shepherd boy could defeat a giant armed with weapons on a battlefield. Yet because of the Lord's faithfulness, that is exactly what happened. I'm sure there was at least one Israelite who thought David was a fool for daring to face that giant. But David's hope was not put to shame.

Another Biblical example that I love is found in 2 Chronicles 20. Jehoshaphat was king and had declared that his people shall serve the Lord. After a time, a large army was on their way to make war against Jehoshaphat. How does Jehoshaphat respond?

"³Jehoshaphat was afraid and turned his attention to seek the Lord, and proclaimed a fast throughout all Judah. ⁴So Judah gathered together to

seek help from the Lord; they even came from all the cities of Judah to seek the Lord.

⁵Then Jehoshaphat stood in the assembly of Judah and Jerusalem, in the house of the Lord before the new court, ⁶and he said, 'O Lord, the God of our fathers, are You not God in the heavens? And are You not ruler over all the kingdoms of the nations? Power and might are in Your hand so that no one can stand against You. ⁷Did You not, O our God, drive out the inhabitants of this land before Your people Israel and give it to the descendants of Abraham Your friend forever? ⁸They have lived in it, and have built You a sanctuary there for Your name, saying, ⁹"Should evil come upon us, the sword, or judgment, or pestilence, or famine, we will stand before this house and before You (for Your name is in this house) and cry to You in our distress, and You will hear and deliver us."

¹⁰Now behold, the sons of Ammon and Moab and Mount Seir, whom You did not let Israel invade when they came out of the land of Egypt (they turned aside from them and did not destroy them), ¹¹see how they are rewarding us by coming to drive us out from Your possession which You have given us as an inheritance. ¹²O our God, will You not judge them? For we are powerless before this great multitude who are coming against us; nor do we know what to do, but our eyes are on You.'

¹³All Judah was standing before the Lord, with their infants, their wives and their children."
2 Chronicles 20:3-13

I love how immediately Jehoshaphat turned to the Lord for help when he was afraid. He also worshiped God, praised Him for His might, and remembered His faithfulness in the past. Then he humbly poured out his fears before the Lord. He basically said, "God, I have no idea what to do...but I trust You." And because of his role as king, not only was Jehoshaphat's heart focused on the Lord, but so were all of the people of Judah. What a wonderful example of leadership and the humility and surrender required to be a good leader!

Jehoshaphat did not know what to do during this time of

suffering. He didn't understand why he was the target of an attack, but he also trusted that he didn't need to know why. He just turned his eyes to God and trusted. He placed his hope in the Lord to help him. And then God answered.

The Spirit of the Lord spoke through one of the listeners and said, *"Do not fear or be dismayed because of this great multitude, for the battle is not yours but God's."* Wow! Can you imagine the chills that ran through the bodies of those who witnessed this?

The Lord continued to give them directions on what to do. He told them to go out to meet them the next day on the battlefield, but *"You need not fight in this battle; station yourselves, stand and see the salvation of the Lord on your behalf, O Judah and Jerusalem. Do not fear or be dismayed; tomorrow go out to face them, for the Lord is with you."*

Come again? Go out to the battlefield, but don't be prepared to fight? Yikes! That seems like a pretty foolish plan to me. This is likely what my reaction would have been. But not theirs. They all bowed down to the Lord and worshiped Him loudly.

Then the next morning, they obeyed the Lord's instructions. As they were going, Jehoshaphat once again displayed admirable leadership by telling the people, *"Listen to me, O Judah and inhabitants of Jerusalem, put your trust in the Lord your God and you will be established. Put your trust in His prophets and succeed."*

He then ordered those whose job it was to sing and praise to go to the front lines and said to all the people, *"Give thanks to the Lord, for His lovingkindness is everlasting."*

Then the miracle happened. God showed up in a big way. When all the people of Judah started singing and worshiping the Lord, the enemies turned on one another and destroyed themselves. It says in verse 24 that their dead bodies were strewn everywhere and that not a single enemy had escaped (I suppose the last person turned the sword on himself).

What a sight that must have been. And there was so much bounty they collected from the dead soldiers that it took them three days to collect it all.

They ended their "battle" the same way it began: worship. The people of Judah turned to the Lord their God in their time of suffering, and they trusted Him with their lives. They trusted Him enough to not even take weapons with them to the battlefield. They just worshiped God. They knew He was good before the battle, during the battle, and after the battle. God is always and only good.

One of my favorite stories in the Old Testament is found in Daniel 3. But for context, I'll back up and summarize Daniel 1 and 2.

Nebuchadnezzar was king of Babylon, and he attacked the people of Judah and took some young men to serve in his kingdom. He ordered that the young men be fed his food, but Daniel and his friends got permission to only eat vegetables. They thrived and were promoted in the kingdom, serving as wise men.

Then Nebuchadnezzar had a disturbing dream that he did not know the meaning of. When all the magicians and conjurers in Babylon couldn't tell him and interpret his dream, he ordered that all the wise men of Babylon be killed (including Daniel and his friends). When Daniel heard about this decree, he and his friends prayed to God to reveal the king's dream and interpretation to him.

That night, God gave Daniel the vision of the king's dream and its interpretation. I love Daniel's response of praise to God after He answered their prayers:

"Then Daniel blessed the God of heaven; 20Daniel said,

'Let the name of God be blessed forever and ever,
For wisdom and power belong to Him.
21It is He who changes the times and the epochs;
He removes kings and establishes kings;
He gives wisdom to wise men
And knowledge to men of understanding.
22It is He who reveals the profound and hidden things;
He knows what is in the darkness,

And the light dwells with Him.
²³To You, O God of my fathers, I give thanks and praise,
For You have given me wisdom and power;
Even now You have made known to me what we requested of You,
For You have made known to us the king's matter.'"
Daniel 2:19-23

They were facing execution, but they trusted God to rescue them by giving Daniel the vision of the king's dream. And God was faithful. I love how Daniel says that God "knows what is in the darkness, and the light dwells with Him." I like to think how this applies to our suffering dark times. God is there. He knows the darkness; every inch of it. Nothing escapes His knowledge. But the light dwells with Him. If we want to escape our darkness, we must seek Him. We must dwell with Him, with the light.

After Daniel received this vision from the Lord, he requested to see the king. Nebuchadnezzar questioned if Daniel was being truthful in his statement that he knew his dream and interpretation. I love Daniel's reply to Nebuchadnezzar:

"²⁷Daniel answered before the king and said, 'As for the mystery about which the king has inquired, neither wise men, conjurers, magicians nor diviners are able to declare it to the king. ²⁸However, there is a God in heaven who reveals mysteries, and He has made known to King Nebuchadnezzar what will take place in the latter days. This was your dream and the visions in your mind while on your bed."
Daniel 2:27-28

Daniel went on to explain Nebuchadnezzar's dream and its interpretation. His dream was about future kingdoms and eventually how God will setup His kingdom on earth, which will never be destroyed like all the previous kingdoms. After Daniel finished speaking...

"⁴⁶Then King Nebuchadnezzar fell on his face and did homage to Daniel, and gave orders to present to him an offering and fragrant incense. ⁴⁷The king answered Daniel and said, 'Surely your God is a God of gods and a Lord of kings and a revealer of mysteries, since you have been able to reveal this mystery.'"

Daniel 2:46-47

Even though Nebuchadnezzar wasn't a believer in God, he still couldn't help but recognize the power and majesty of Him. The king promoted Daniel and his friends and gave them gifts and prestige.

But Nebuchadnezzar didn't stay in awe of God for long. In Daniel 3, Nebuchadnezzar built a 90-foot golden statue as an idol and commanded that all the people in Babylon worship it, or they would be thrown into the furnace and killed. Goodness, Nebuchadnezzar seemed like a very angry man of extremes and overreactions, as you will continue to see examples of.

Some tattletales went and told Nebuchadnezzar about Daniel's friends who were refusing to worship the golden statue. (I'm not sure why Daniel wasn't told on as well, but nonetheless, Daniel 3 focuses on his friends.) His friends' names were Hananiah (renamed Shadrach by the Babylonians), Mishael (renamed Meshach), and Azariah (renamed Abed-nego).

When Nebuchadnezzar was told about these three refusing to worship his golden statue, Nebuchadnezzar was "in rage and anger" and ordered that they be brought before him. When they were brought before him, he asked them if what he heard was true. He gave them one more chance: worship the golden statue or "you will immediately be cast into the midst of a furnace of blazing fire; and what god is there who can deliver you out of my hands?" I love their reply:

"¹⁶Shadrach, Meshach and Abed-nego replied to the king, 'O Nebuchadnezzar, we do not need to give you an answer concerning this

matter. ¹⁷If it be so, our God whom we serve is able to deliver us from the furnace of blazing fire; and He will deliver us out of your hand, O king. ¹⁸But even if He does not, let it be known to you, O king, that we are not going to serve your gods or worship the golden image that you have set up."'
Daniel 3:16-18

Wow, what guts that took! Rather, what faith that required. They were standing next to a hot furnace as the king questioned them, and they fully knew their choices. How amazing their trust in the Lord was! They told Nebuchadnezzar that their God is able to make the impossible possible, but that even if He didn't, they would still only worship Him. This is a marvelous example to us during trials and suffering: God is good and deserving of our trust and faithfulness. Even if the suffering continues. Even if the answer is no. Even if the outcome is death. He is worthy.

In verse 19 it is said that Nebuchadnezzar "was filled with wrath, and his facial expression was altered toward Shadrach, Meshach and Abed-nego. He answered by giving orders to heat the furnace seven times more than it was usually heated." Yeah, I think it's safe to say that Nebuchadnezzar was a hothead and would have benefited from some anger management sessions.

The furnace was so hot that the men Nebuchadnezzar ordered to tie up Shadrach, Meshach and Abed-nego and then throw them into the furnace were burned up and slain. Verse 23 says that "Shadrach, Meshach and Abed-nego, fell into the midst of the furnace of blazing fire still tied up." This next part gives me chills.

"²⁴Then Nebuchadnezzar the king was astounded and stood up in haste; he said to his high officials, 'Was it not three men we cast bound into the midst of the fire?' They replied to the king, 'Certainly, O king.' ²⁵He said, 'Look! I see four men loosed and walking about in the midst of the fire without harm, and the appearance of the fourth is like a son of the gods!' ²⁶Then Nebuchadnezzar came near to the door of the furnace of blazing fire; he responded and said, 'Shadrach, Meshach and Abed-nego,

come out, you servants of the Most High God, and come here!' Then Shadrach, Meshach and Abed-nego came out of the midst of the fire. *²⁷The satraps, the prefects, the governors and the king's high officials gathered around and saw in regard to these men that the fire had no effect on the bodies of these men nor was the hair of their head singed, nor were their trousers damaged, nor had the smell of fire even come upon them.*

²⁸Nebuchadnezzar responded and said, 'Blessed be the God of Shadrach, Meshach and Abed-nego, who has sent His angel and delivered His servants who put their trust in Him, violating the king's command, and yielded up their bodies so as not to serve or worship any god except their own God. ²⁹Therefore I make a decree that any people, nation or tongue that speaks anything offensive against the God of Shadrach, Meshach and Abed-nego shall be torn limb from limb and their houses reduced to a rubbish heap, inasmuch as there is no other god who is able to deliver in this way.' ³⁰Then the king caused Shadrach, Meshach and Abed-nego to prosper in the province of Babylon."
Daniel 3:24-30

I love the imagery in this section of Scripture. Nebuchadnezzar was so surprised and astounded that he jumped up. Not a hair on their heads, nor a thread on their clothing, was singed. Not a hint of the smell of smoke was found on them, but the ropes that they had been bound with were gone since Nebuchadnezzar saw their figures "loosed and walking about in the midst of the fire without harm." And they weren't alone. Nebuchadnezzar also saw a fourth figure in the flames, One whose appearance "is like a son of the gods." Jesus was with them! How amazing is that?

When your suffering makes you feel like you're surrounded by flames in a burning furnace, remember that Jesus is with you. He has removed the ropes of sin that once bound you to this world and the enemy. You are loosed and freely walking about in the kingdom of God. You are His beloved child, and He is Your Savior. Trust Him. Trust Him through the fire.

I love how Nebuchadnezzar acknowledged God's might and majesty after what he witnessed. He walked to the furnace door and asked them to come out of the furnace, calling them "servants of the Most High God." After seeing that they were unharmed, he praised God and recognized that God "delivered His servants who put their trust in Him."

Even after Nebuchadnezzar's rule was over and a different king, Darius, was ruler of Babylon, God continued to display his glory and might. Daniel once again had been distinguished among all the others working in his kingdom, and Darius had grown very fond of Daniel. The others serving in the kingdom didn't like that, so they plotted against Daniel. They convinced King Darius to institute a law that anyone who worshiped anyone other than him was to be thrown into a lions' den. Darius, not knowing that Daniel would be caught disobeying this law, agreed to it. Their evil plan worked, and they caught Daniel worshiping God and brought Daniel before King Darius. Darius was deeply troubled but had to carry out the punishment of the law.

Verse 16 says, "Then the king gave orders, and Daniel was brought in and cast into the lions' den. The king spoke and said to Daniel, 'Your God whom you constantly serve will Himself deliver you.'"

"18Then the king went off to his palace and spent the night fasting, and no entertainment was brought before him; and his sleep fled from him.

19Then the king arose at dawn, at the break of day, and went in haste to the lions' den. 20When he had come near the den to Daniel, he cried out with a troubled voice. The king spoke and said to Daniel, 'Daniel, servant of the living God, has your God, whom you constantly serve, been able to deliver you from the lions?' 21Then Daniel spoke to the king, 'O king, live forever! 22My God sent His angel and shut the lions' mouths and they have not harmed me, inasmuch as I was found innocent before Him; and also toward you, O king, I have committed no crime.' 23Then the king was very pleased and gave orders for Daniel to be taken up out of the den. So Daniel was taken up out of the den and no injury whatever was found on him, because he had trusted in his God. 24The king then gave orders, and they brought those men who had maliciously accused

Daniel, and they cast them, their children and their wives into the lions'
den; and they had not reached the bottom of the den before the lions
overpowered them and crushed all their bones."
Daniel 6:18-24

I thought it was sweet how Darius worried all night on behalf of Daniel. And I love how in verse 23 it says that he was saved from the lions "because he had trusted in his God." That's not the end of God getting the glory.

"25Then Darius the king wrote to all the peoples, nations and men of every
language who were living in all the land: 'May your peace abound! 26I
make a decree that in all the dominion of my kingdom men are to fear and
tremble before the God of Daniel;

For He is the living God and enduring forever,
And His kingdom is one which will not be destroyed,
And His dominion will be forever.
27 He delivers and rescues and performs signs and wonders
In heaven and on earth,
Who has also delivered Daniel from the power of the lions.'"
Daniel 6:25-27

Daniel and his friends were taken from their home and forced into serving a king who was not their own, who worshiped gods who were not their own. They were brought through trial after trial as they served and faced death a couple times, and yet God was glorified time and time again. Their suffering served a purpose, and their hope in the Lord was not in vain. The same is true for you.

❧

A couple of weeks after we had Abby put to sleep, the thought "*Your body is healed and your womb is open*" kept entering my mind. This was a very strange thing for me to think. We were over six years into our time of infertility, and I had accepted that I might never get pregnant and felt peace about that. We were also on the waiting list with a local adoption agency to hopefully be chosen by a birth mother and bring a second baby into our home.

But that thought would not go away. Over the next couple of weeks, I began to feel peace about being open to some fertility treatments, something I had never felt peace about before. I also saw a random article about something I hadn't heard of before called embryo adoption. It's when couples that did an IVF treatment but didn't transfer all the viable embryos can choose to relinquish those embryos for other couples to adopt and transfer in hopes of getting pregnant. We were already comfortable adopting a child that I didn't carry in my womb, but the idea that maybe we could experience pregnancy in addition to adoption was appealing to me.

Around mid-February, I decided that I should talk to Michael about all of these thoughts that had been on my mind so he would know where my heart was at. To my surprise, he said that he too had been thinking recently about feeling open to fertility treatments – something he too had never felt peace about before (and it was also very unlike him to think much about family planning in general with all the hobbies and interests he regularly has on his mind). When I brought up the idea of embryo adoption, he felt peace about that too.

He also marveled at how far God had brought us in our journey. The idea of embryo adoption was something he would have never come around to without God's doing because the very idea of "another man's sperm" (in the form of an embryo) being transferred into his wife was one of the most humbling things he could imagine. Yet he felt peace about it and wanted to trust God to see where this new peace would take us.

Feeling surprised and excited that we were on the same page about this topic, we scheduled an appointment with a fertility specialist to begin the process of some basic treatments and then embryo adoption as an option afterwards. We made the appointment for March 21st.

On March 7th, Michael was home for lunch, and I was

cleaning the toilet in our bathroom. I was alone in the bathroom and started thinking about how I was three days past when I should have started my period. It had been my habit for over six years to hope and wonder if maybe I was finally pregnant each month. Sometimes I would use an at-home pregnancy test, but I hadn't in years because it was just too discouraging to always see a negative result.

But being three days late was unusual for me, and I kept debating with myself all morning if I should use a pregnancy test or not. Finally around lunch time, after I cleaned the toilet, I decided to just do it. If it was negative, then I could stop wondering if I was pregnant and stop thinking about being a little bit late.

In the past when I would complete a pregnancy test, I would wait the three minutes you're supposed to and then strain my eyes and hold the test under the brightest light in the house to hopefully, maybe, see the faintest of a second line. In all the pregnancy tests I used, a second line had never appeared.

But on this day, before I could even set the test strip down to begin waiting the three minutes, a bold second line had already appeared.

To say I felt shocked was an understatement. I remember staring at the two lines for a few seconds, blinking several times to see if it was just my imagination or dry contact lenses. But it wasn't. There were clearly two lines on the pregnancy test.

In that moment of shock, I didn't quite know what to do. I just kept holding onto the positive pregnancy test. Some wives are capable of keeping news like that to themselves for a while and then find some clever way to tell their husbands, but I am not that type of wife. My approach was to immediately run out of the bathroom with the positive test and into the living room to show Michael.

But he wasn't in the living room where I last saw him. I then heard Elizabeth crying from her bedroom and thought, "Maybe he's in her room comforting her." I then saw his cell phone sitting on the counter, so I grabbed it real quick and began recording video.

Sure enough, Michael was in Elizabeth's room sitting on the floor hugging and rocking her to soothe her. I entered the room with the positive test behind my back and said in a shaky voice, "Hey honey, I just, uh, need to tell you something." I pulled the test strip out from behind my back, held it up for him to see, and said, "This is why I haven't started my period." He looked at me in shock and said, "What does that mean?" (He says he didn't want to jump to the wrong conclusion without being sure of how to respond.) I said, "I'm pregnant."

I then began to sob with joy and felt overwhelmed with the idea of how good God is. We hugged and cried and praised the Lord for His goodness. We didn't know if this pregnancy would go to term, but we wanted to rejoice for the gift of that day no matter how things turned out. We decided to share this news with friends and family right from the beginning because we wanted to rejoice in what God had done. If I ended up miscarrying, we would face that suffering at that time, but this was the time to rejoice.

❦

Hope doesn't always have to make sense. Hoping in dire situations may result in others thinking you a fool, but hope in Christ never leads to shame. Hope sustains you, drives you, and carries you through suffering.

CHAPTER 10
Your Worth

My love for horses continued well into adulthood. When I started college, I was no longer taking weekly horse lessons, but I still desired to ride whenever I could. Without owning my own horse, I had to get creative. There was a student club that related to horses, and every six weeks or so they offered a free riding clinic where you could ride one of the school-owned horses. As a college student who enjoyed sleeping in late on the weekends, a chance to ride a horse was well worth the sacrifice of a Saturday morning's sleep.

At a Saturday riding clinic in the spring semester, one of the students leading the clinic suggested that I try out for the equestrian team that she was on. She told me about the upcoming spring date for the team's open tryouts to join the team that fall semester. I didn't know much about it, but I decided to give it a try and hope for the best.

I felt like I did okay during the tryouts but felt out of riding shape (because I was since I wasn't taking lessons and didn't ride regularly). Riding once every six weeks is not enough to stay in shape. But I tried out, and I was happy with that.

I was disappointed but not too surprised when I received an email thanking me for trying out but that the team would not be able to offer me a spot in the fall. I was still glad I tried out though. I put it behind me and enjoyed my summer.

Late in the summer, I was very surprised and confused when I received an email congratulating me for being called back for tryouts at the beginning of the fall semester. Was this a mistake? A clerical error?

I showed up at the fall tryouts and did my best, hoping that the little bit of riding I was able to do at my aunt's that summer had served me well. A couple of days later, I received an email congratulating me for making the equestrian team and asking me to report for the fall semester orientation. Could this really be happening?

I decided to show up at the orientation as instructed, but to be completely honest, a big part of me wondered if I would show up, the coaches would realize they had made a huge mistake, and I wasn't supposed to have been offered a spot on the team after all.

But that fear was unrealized – they had paperwork and official team clothing prepared for me with my name on it. I felt so honored to be part of a team, even if I barely made the cut. After all, this meant that I received benefits of being an NCAA athlete like having a physical trainer design our workouts. And I got to ride horses three times a week!

It was a lot of hard work, especially balancing team commitments on top of my engineering workload and a part-time job. But it was worth it.

The team was really talented and performed very well at the competitions. I learned a lot while on the equestrian team and became a more confident rider, but I was never selected to compete for the team. Although I was grateful to have been a part of the team for two years, I never felt like I was "enough" to belong. I felt like all the other ladies were prettier than me, rode better than me, had been riding longer than me, owned their own horse, and were stronger than me.

These feelings added more baggage to my lifelong struggles with self-confidence. The message "you're not enough" was a lie that was deeply embedded in my heart and still threatens to spring up to this day. Those deep heart lies can be so difficult to uproot.

I bet you also have some deep heart lies that you have believed your whole life, lies that were born out of childhood trauma, the enemy, or your own fears, insecurities, or habits.

What are the deep heart lies that you believe?

I believe that it is critical for your spiritual, emotional, and physical health to identify those lies and counteract them with Truth (see chapter 6). Your worth is found in Jesus.

❦

Seeing the first ultrasound at seven weeks pregnant was incredible. Our baby was really in there, moving, and had a strong heartbeat. Learning that our baby was a girl at the 20-week ultrasound was a joyous time. I felt her move. I wasn't sure at first if it was my imagination or not, but eventually I learned when it was her. My stomach grew and grew. Even before she was born, she and I started getting to know one another. She would get the hiccups at least once a day. She liked to move the most in the evenings and slept soundly through the night.

Apparently she liked it so much in there that she did not want to come out. Desiring a natural birth if possible, I waited and waited…and waited. After having my membrane stripped twice, being 100% effaced, and almost 4 cm dilated for an entire week without going into active labor, I finally agreed to be induced at 42 weeks and 2 days pregnant.

Even though I was induced, I was grateful that my labor was very short because I did it all without pain interventions. It was three hours from the onset of painful contractions to our daughter being born. Our sweet Katherine was born and made our family grow from three to four.

Elizabeth was the miracle who made me a mom and came with a wonderful, loving birth family. Katherine was the miracle that gave me the gift of experiencing pregnancy, breastfeeding, and raising a biological child who looks so much like her daddy. Both miracles are treasures from God, and we can't believe sometimes that God saw fit to make us their parents. Such good gifts.

❦

Whether life gives you lemons or lemonade, you are the one who chooses your response. I encourage you to choose hope and joy. Your feelings ebb and flow, but your attitude is your choice. Choosing hope and joy does not preclude you from feeling sad.

Yes, your attitude is your choice, but also recognize that everyone makes poor choices sometimes. We all have bad days. We all have days where nothing goes our way, we're exhausted, out of patience, the car won't start, and you realize you had something stuck in your teeth all day long and no one told you. Give yourself grace for those inevitable moments. You don't have to meet God's standard of perfection because you can't. That's why you need Jesus; He could and did. His grace is freely given to those who accept it, both for eternal salvation and the day-to-day living. In those hard moments where you catch yourself despairing again, messing up again, lashing out in anger again...just stop. Stop and thank Him for His grace. Accept it and move forward.

"Brethren, I do not regard myself as having laid hold of it yet; but one thing I do: forgetting what lies behind and reaching forward to what lies ahead, I press on toward the goal for the prize of the upward call of God in Christ Jesus."
Philippians 3:13-14

It's important to also remember that you're not the only one who has bad days and ugly moments. When someone says something insensitive to you, minimizes your suffering, offers unsolicited advice, or cuts you off on your way to the store, remember that they likely did not wake up that morning with the sole intent of getting under your skin. People say hurtful things. People fail to show up sometimes. People make mistakes and let you down sometimes. The same grace that is freely offered to you is also offered to others. And because of that, you are asked to offer that grace to others too.

"¹²So, as those who have been chosen of God, holy and beloved, put on a heart of compassion, kindness, humility, gentleness and patience; ¹³bearing with one another, and forgiving each other, whoever has a complaint against anyone; just as the Lord forgave you, so also should you. ¹⁴Beyond all these things put on love, which is the perfect bond of unity. ¹⁵Let the peace of Christ rule in your hearts, to which indeed you were called in one body; and be thankful. ¹⁶Let the word of Christ richly dwell within you, with all wisdom teaching and admonishing one another with psalms and hymns and spiritual songs, singing with thankfulness in your hearts to God. ¹⁷Whatever you do in word or deed, do all in the name of the Lord Jesus, giving thanks through Him to God the Father."
Colossians 3:12-17

We get grace, and we give grace. We are all precious to our Father. You are so loved by God that He subjected Himself to a life of suffering. He left His throne to offer you a place in His kingdom. He knew He would face a painful, tortuous death, but He chose to endure it anyway for you, His precious child.

He sees your worth. He sees your pain and is there with you through it. He sees your worst, and He embraces you wholeheartedly. It doesn't get any better than that.

When you experience suffering, you have a wonderful opportunity to point back to Christ. You have a wonderful opportunity to share all of the ways God has given you grace through your suffering and how you have been able to give grace and encouragement to others because of it. Our suffering and our brokenness always leads back to Jesus. To God be the glory, forever and ever, amen.

The more life you live, the more pain and suffering you will experience. Time is unforgiving in that way. Time is unstoppable, inevitable, and binds this sin-riddled world in which we live. But time also gives you a gift of opportunity. You have the opportunity to know God more and more throughout your life if you choose to seek Him. His Word is true and alive. His ear is always ready to listen. His eyes always see. His arms always ready to embrace. His Spirit always ready to guide. His heart always yours to keep.

He is worth getting to know if you haven't already started. And in my experience, I find the most comfort in knowing Him when I experience trials and suffering. I love looking for all the little ways that He speaks to me and reassures me of His presence and love. He is all around us: in nature, in our prayers, working through loved ones, smiling at us through our children, in the way he designed your dog to somehow sense when you feel sad and know to come and snuggle with you. He wants to know you deeply and intimately. He wants to carry you through whatever you're facing. He wants you to know that you are not alone.

If you learn only one thing from this book, I pray it is this: **God deeply loves and cares for you and wants to carry your burdens. He is worthy of your trust.**

The better you know Him, the easier it will be for you to trust Him with every aspect of your life. The longer you live, the more opportunities you will have to make that choice. Surrender to Him and trust Him. You don't have to carry your burdens, your fears, or your pain alone. Surrender all to Him.

No matter what your suffering is, all you need is Christ. Even if like Job everything you have and everyone you love is taken away from you, all you need is Jesus. He is your hope and your foundation.

⊙〜❧〜⊙

Elizabeth has always been independent and very driven. She was early on all her physical milestones. She did not have time to cuddle because there was a world out there to figure out. She loves to be included in whatever we're doing and loves to ask lots of questions. She has an amazing memory and loves learning new things. She is a natural leader and administrator. We joke that with her advanced negotiating and arguing skills she should pursue being a lawyer.

Katherine is my cuddle bug. She loves to be held and will lean her forehead towards you if you ask for a kiss. She used to tuck her head under my chin when I held her and sang to her before putting her to bed. During her first year, she was quiet and content, not driven to accomplish anything until she decided she was ready. She didn't start crawling until after 12 months old but then quickly progressed through the rest of the physical milestones to keep up with her big sister. Now she is a typical energetic toddler but still has a sweet, nurturing character trait.

It's been such a joy to raise two adorable, yet very unique little girls. They love each other so much (at least for now, and I pray that continues through the years). Ever since our struggles with infertility began, we have desired to have as many children as God wants to give us, either biologically or through adoption. Getting pregnant with Katherine was such an unexpected answer to prayer, and it also reignited hope that perhaps more biological children are in God's plan for our family.

Elizabeth loves being a big sister so much that she also wanted to expand her responsibilities. For many months she prayed that God would give her a baby brother.

Fourteen months after Katherine was born, I found out I was pregnant. When I got the positive result on the pregnancy test strip, I repeated the same method from the previous time: I grabbed my cell phone and caught on video me telling Michael that I was pregnant again. This time Elizabeth was old enough to understand the concept, so I also caught on video us telling her that God may have answered her prayer, that I was pregnant with her baby brother or sister. We were all so excited.

I quickly entered the nauseous phase of the first trimester and battled finding foods and avoiding smells that didn't make me gag. Overall, my nausea wasn't quite as bad as it was when I was pregnant with Katherine, which made me wonder if perhaps Elizabeth's prayer really would be answered, that perhaps I was pregnant with a boy.

About a month later, Michael and I were relaxing one evening watching TV. I had to pee, again, like pregnancy hormones make you do. But when I went to bathroom, I saw bright, red blood. Too much blood to be considered spotting. It was just like it would look if I had suddenly started my period. Panic rushed through my body and mind. I quickly prayed and asked God to protect our baby. I tried to hold onto the hope that maybe this was still within the normal range for spotting.

But the bleeding continued and got a little heavier. I decided that the most important thing for me to do was to stay calm, and I knew a trip to the ER would result in so much stress and anxiety. If I was miscarrying, there was nothing the ER could do. I decided to wait until the next morning and go see my doctor as soon as possible.

I didn't sleep much at all that night. I went to sleep crying, praying, and hoping. I drifted off a couple times, but every time I woke up, I would remember what I was facing and start crying, praying, and hoping again. Never has a night felt so long.

I called the doctor's office as soon as they opened. My usual doctor was out of town, but one of her partners was available to see me for an ultrasound that morning. My parents came over to stay with our girls while Michael drove me to the doctor's office. We sat in the waiting room, mostly quiet, but also anxious.

They called us back. The doctor brought in the ultrasound machine. She squirted the cold gel on my stomach and began looking for the baby. She looked for a long time. Gently, she said she didn't see a baby, just cloudiness which could be clots. She said I may have already passed the baby or it may be hidden behind the clots. Either way, it was not a healthy pregnancy. She had suffered miscarriages herself and was very sympathetic and kind. She told me in detail what I could expect.

I managed to hold it together for the most part in the office, but as soon as we got back in the car, I broke down. It was such a strange feeling. There was no longer a life in my womb, but that little one's body might still be in there. It was a mixture of dread of what was still to come but also relief that now at least I knew that our little one was with Jesus, even if his or her body remained. I felt sad and empty. But I still trusted God and thanked Him for His mercy that because of Jesus, I have hope that one day I will get to meet my little one in heaven.

When we arrived at home, we came inside and had to tell Elizabeth what had happened. I will never forget that moment. She's always been very intelligent and mature for her age. She was four years old at the time. I squatted down, looked her in the eyes with tears in mine and gently said, "We lost the baby." She immediately understood and began to cry. This made both of us cry more, and we all just hugged one another. I kept telling her that the baby is in heaven with Jesus, and that we just need to keep praying. She continued to feel sad and talk about her feelings for the next several months. She continued to pray for another baby brother.

During those long hours the night before, struggling to sleep, something kept coming into my mind: the story of Hannah. Hannah was one of two wives to a man named Elkanah. His other wife had several children, but Hannah's womb was closed. The other wife would harass and tease Hannah for her affliction.

"¹⁰She, greatly distressed, prayed to the Lord and wept bitterly. ¹¹She made a vow and said, 'O Lord of hosts, if You will indeed look on the affliction of Your maidservant and remember me, and not forget Your maidservant, but will give Your maidservant a son, then I will give him to the Lord all the days of his life, and a razor shall never come on his head.'

¹²Now it came about, as she continued praying before the Lord, that Eli was watching her mouth. ¹³As for Hannah, she was speaking in her heart, only her lips were moving, but her voice was not heard. So Eli thought she was drunk. ¹⁴Then Eli said to her, 'How long will you make yourself drunk? Put away your wine from you.' ¹⁵But Hannah replied, 'No, my lord, I am a woman oppressed in spirit; I have drunk neither wine nor strong drink, but I have poured out my soul before the Lord.

¹⁶Do not consider your maidservant as a worthless woman, for I have spoken until now out of my great concern and provocation.' ¹⁷Then Eli answered and said, 'Go in peace; and may the God of Israel grant your petition that you have asked of Him.' ¹⁸She said, 'Let your maidservant find favor in your sight.' So the woman went her way and ate, and her face was no longer sad.

¹⁹Then they arose early in the morning and worshiped before the Lord, and returned again to their house in Ramah. And Elkanah had relations with Hannah his wife, and the Lord remembered her. ²⁰It came about in due time, after Hannah had conceived, that she gave birth to a son; and she named him Samuel, saying, 'Because I have asked him of the Lord.'

²⁴Now when she had weaned him, she took him up with her, with a three-year-old bull and one ephah of flour and a jug of wine, and brought him to the house of the Lord in Shiloh, although the child was young. ²⁵Then they slaughtered the bull, and brought the boy to Eli. ²⁶She said, 'Oh, my lord! As your soul lives, my lord, I am the woman who stood here beside you, praying to the Lord. ²⁷For this boy I prayed, and the Lord has given me my petition which I asked of Him. ²⁸So I have also dedicated him to the Lord; as long as he lives he is dedicated to the Lord.' And he worshiped the Lord there."
1 Samuel 1:10-28

I can relate to this story in so many ways. I can relate to the loneliness and despair that Hannah felt when she poured her heart out to God in anguish, begging for Him to remember her. I can picture the scene of Eli mistaking this woman for a drunk and then realizing that he had just met a broken woman. She left everything she had on the steps of that temple. She had surrendered everything to God, trusting Him to rescue her. And because of her faith, she went away in confidence and no longer with a sad face.

Faith isn't a guarantee of fortune. Hannah's faith wasn't a guarantee that she would conceive, but in this story, that is what happened. Hannah conceived and had a son she named Samuel. And then, after all that time, and pain, and anguish, and hope, and prayers…she surrendered Samuel to God. She gave him away to the Lord. Love is sacrifice, and that is what Hannah did. She sacrificed the opportunity to watch Samuel grow up and to raise him. She trusted the Lord with him.

Because Elizabeth had been praying for a baby brother, we decided to think of that baby as a boy, even though we never learned the gender. We named him Samuel because like Hannah, we gave him back to the Lord.

It took three months for my hormones to settle after the miscarriage and four months after that to conceive again. But that conception didn't last either – I miscarried at four weeks, which was when my period was due. They call it a chemical pregnancy, as if that somehow makes it any less of a baby. It was still a life that was lost. Even though I only knew about the pregnancy for two days, it was still hard. I could have known about it for only two seconds and still mourned for what I knew I was losing. The hope of knowing that little one, seeing what he/she looked like, or who God would shape them to be.

It was tempting to think that this pregnancy wasn't real or didn't count, but life begins at conception. And since scientists discovered that there's a flash of light at the moment sperm joins egg, I decided to name this little life Celeste because it reminded me of light.

Losing these two little lives was so painful. I heard something extremely encouraging from a podcast about pregnancy losses, and in case you have suffered a similar loss, I want to share it with you too. The idea was this: if we are each created to be worshippers of God, then how special and marvelous it is that your womb played a role in creating yet another worshiper of God.

Had it not been for my faith in God and His goodness, demonstrated through all the years of infertility through His faithfulness in working good into my pain, I think I would have been pulled down into despair and self-blame for my miscarriages. Friends, the enemy is set on destroying you, and he will seize every opportunity to do so. He will use a tragedy completely out of your control, somehow twist it around to make you feel like whatever bad thing is happening to you is all your fault, and you deserve it. He is a wretched enemy but very clever and capable. This is why dependence on Christ as your firm foundation and your source for strength, hope, grace, forgiveness, endurance, and perseverance is critical to this life.

We cannot avoid experiencing suffering, but we can place our hope and trust in the One who is greater and more powerful than anything that could potentially hurt us. He is worthy.

❧

The Truth really will set you free. And the Truth is found in Jesus. Your worth is found in Christ. Remember that 1 Corinthians 1:30 says, "But by His doing you are in Christ Jesus, who became to us wisdom from God, and righteousness and sanctification, and redemption." Jesus is your wisdom from God. Jesus is your righteousness. Jesus is your sanctification. And Jesus is your redemption.

Jesus took every single wrong, mistake, and shameful thing you've ever done or ever will do, and he died for it. Once and for all. Your sin died, but Jesus revived. Your very sin nature was crucified as well, and you are now a saint who sometimes sins. If you have trusted in Christ's sacrifice for your sin, then when God looks at you, He sees Jesus. You are loved. You are cherished. You are valuable. You are redeemed. You are His child. Forever, no matter what you do, no matter how much suffering you endure. You are seen. You are His.

If you can adopt this belief as the new deep message of your heart instead of the lies, then you will be ready when life's storms come your way. You will be ready to choose hope.

EPILOGUE

After the year of two pregnancy losses and no medical explanation for them, we decided to pursue IUI fertility treatments as the next step. At the beginning of 2020, we met with a doctor to learn more about the procedure. Since there was still a question about whether or not my body produced enough progesterone to sustain a pregnancy, we decided to get a baseline progesterone test before doing our first cycle of IUI. That blood test was drawn a week after I believe I ovulated. To our surprise, my progesterone was the highest it had ever been, and I wasn't supplementing with progesterone anymore. We took that as a good sign that I don't need to supplement it, and we felt ready to do an IUI on the next cycle.

But God had a different plan: we actually conceived naturally that cycle, which could explain why the progesterone result was so high. I had my blood tested a few times over a period of a couple of weeks to confirm that HCG and progesterone were both rising.

At five weeks, I started spotting a little, which immediately triggered my anxiety from the previous two losses. I went in for an ultrasound, and thankfully, the sonographer saw a healthy looking yolk and gestational sac.

Fear and anxiety were a constant struggle for me during this pregnancy, especially up until the gestational age that I lost Samuel. I shared the news with my closest friends and family, but no one else. They prayed for and encouraged me over the weeks. Whenever I felt the fear and anxiety threatening to take over, I read Philippians 4:4-8 over and over.

I routinely felt God's peace wash over me, encouraging me to let go of control and trust Him with this baby. He convicted me that I was letting the outcome of this pregnancy determine my worldview. Instead, I needed to trust God, no matter how this pregnancy turned out. This conviction continued literally through the entire pregnancy, as you will soon see.

But first I want to share some sweet ways that God

encouraged me when I felt overwhelmed with fear and anxiety. The first occasion was shortly after I first found out I was pregnant. I was getting my blood tested every couple of days to make sure HCG was rising as it should. I was feeling anxious as I drove to the lab, but then I noticed that I happened to be stopped behind a car that had a muddy back window and a sticker on the window that said "faith." I immediately thought about how realistic to life that is: we must often have faith, even when life is messy or the future is clouded and unknown. I thought it was so sweet of my God to arrange it such that I happened to be behind that car at just the right time.

The second occasion was when I was five weeks and started spotting a little. Before I could get the ultrasound, the doctor wanted to check my HCG levels to see if the ultrasound would be able to reveal anything. As I sat in the waiting room of the lab, I struggled with feeling anxious but tried to calm myself by reading those Philippians verses. A man walked in, and I overheard him tell the receptionist, "My name is David...my date of birth is October 17th..." The reason this caught my attention is because David has been my favorite boy name ever since Michael and I started dating. And my calculated due date (at that time) was October 17th. I couldn't believe what I'd heard. I even spoke to the man and asked him to repeat his name, then played it off like I mistook him for someone else so as not to come across as a crazy person. But after he left, I sat there in awe of my God. Of all the labs in town, of all the times of day, of all the male names, and of all the birth dates possible, that man with that name and birth date walked into the one I was sitting in at that moment. I went from feeling overwhelmed with fear to feeling overwhelmed with love. My God made me feel like He can do anything, He sees me, and He just wanted to send me a sweet message to remind me to trust in Him. I felt "the peace of God, which surpasses all comprehension" fill my mind and heart.

A little over a week later, the third occasion happened. I was about six weeks pregnant and still spotting off and on. My ultrasounds and blood tests were all normal, but I still struggled to let go of fear and trust God with this pregnancy. It felt like I had to keep surrendering every other second of every day. As I drove to the grocery store, I was listening to our local Christian radio station. At the time, the *For King & Country* song "Burn the Ships" was a new favorite of mine. I prayed and asked God to let that song play on the radio because I wanted it to encourage me. I parked at the store and did my shopping. After finishing, I turned the car on to head back home. As soon as the radio came on, "Burn the Ships" started playing, from the beginning, right then. It wasn't unusual for that song to play on a Christian radio station, but to have it begin playing right at that moment when I was ready to drive home is what made me feel overwhelmed again with God's love for me. Yet again, He saw me, cared for me, and answered my little prayer asking for that song to encourage me.

God didn't have to encourage me in any of the ways that He did, but He wanted to. He knew each of those occasions would matter to me in a big way. He knows me so intimately and delights in me that He wanted to encourage me in those ways. I'm so thankful for His love for me. He feels the same way about you and desires for you to seek and trust Him with your life and circumstances too.

My pregnancy continued healthily. We learned the gender at ten weeks from a blood test: another girl! At my 20-week ultrasound, baby girl looked perfectly healthy. The only concern noted was that my placenta was partially covering my cervix (marginal placenta previa). Because of that issue, I had many more ultrasounds during the third trimester than what is typical. This is another example of God's plans being better than my own. Around 32 weeks, my midwife and the sonographer noted that while my placenta had moved out of the way to allow for a vaginal delivery, the umbilical cord was bundled together and located between her head and my cervix. This is called funic presentation. Funic presentation doesn't always but often can result in a cord prolapsing during labor, which is life-threatening to the baby because their head compresses the cord, cutting off their supply of oxygen. Stillbirths or brain damage are a common outcome of cord prolapses that go undetected.

Because the funic presentation was caught early, it allowed us to research the issue and make a safe plan for our baby girl's delivery. I tried doing some inversions to hopefully give some extra room for the cord to move out of the way, but it didn't work. I also saw a maternal fetal medicine specialist, who said that she doesn't recommend trying for a vaginal birth because there was so much cord bundled there. She said normally with funic presentation it may just be one portion of the cord in the way, which could potentially be slid out of the way in labor. But she said my case is a little bit rare in that the placenta happened to attach where it did, the cord insertion location happened to be on the low side of the placenta, and it happened to angle downward toward the cervix, creating the situation I had where all the excess cord was bundled together like a phone cord between baby's head and my cervix.

Back to God using this entire pregnancy to convict me to surrender my plans and trust Him. A c-section was definitely not my plan. I wanted a natural vaginal birth, but in this situation, it was clear that my plan was not safe to pursue because it could literally be the difference between life or death for our daughter. God helped me to again let go of my grip of control and trust Him. There was nothing I did to cause my situation and there was nothing I could do to change it. But by His graciousness, he allowed for us to discover this high-risk situation early enough to plan for a c-section delivery at 39 weeks.

Our baby girl grew a little bit more, but her growth stalled around 35 weeks, likely because her weight was starting to put some pressure on the cord, limiting its ability to give her the nutrients she needed to keep growing at the same rate. We scheduled the c-section two days shy of 39 weeks. I was so terrified right before the surgery. The anesthesiologist came in to tell me about all the medications she would use, the possible side effects, what medications she would use to counter the side effects, on and on…I felt overwhelmed and began crying as soon as she left. I had never had major surgery before, so the unknowns added to my nervousness. I hated having to do things so unnaturally, but of course I knew that in this situation there really was no other option in order to protect my baby girl.

I'm thankful for all the ways my friends, family, and Michael encouraged me leading up to this moment. They prayed for me and reminded me to trust God.

Right before they started the surgery, I felt peace come over me. I felt loved by God, and all those praying for and thinking of me.

Our sweet Eleanor was born small for her gestational age (a little over 5 pounds) but has been showing the world how tough she is ever since she was born. She was eager to nurse often, very quiet and content, loves to lock eyes with people, and has such a joyful demeanor. She's a ray of sunshine in our family, and we're so thankful that God protected her and allowed her to be a part of it on this side of heaven.

I'm still a work in progress in so many ways. I still have plenty of moments where I think I have more control over my life than I actually do. I still try to make plans and struggle when life doesn't follow them. I still get angry and speak harshly to my children. I still behave selfishly, pridefully, dishonestly, immorally…I really could go on, but I think you get the idea. I still sometimes sin, but I know deep in my heart that that's not my identity anymore. I know how much I sin, but I am redeemed because I trusted in Christ's sacrifice on the cross to pay the penalty for each and every one. Because of that choice, I am called a child of God. I am forever His, and He is forever My Father. No matter what suffering this life holds, I hold onto the hope and promise that one day, all sin, death, and suffering will be put to an end. You can have that same hope too. I promise you that it will not disappoint.

ABOUT THE AUTHOR

Christine Yager writes about her life, marriage, infertility, adoption, and parenting journey, and all the ways that God has worked throughout. She has a passion for encouraging others to trust Christ no matter the circumstances or suffering endured. She has shared her story on podcasts and at women's events, and is always open to additional speaking opportunities to share what God has done through her story. Christine and her family live in Texas.

Made in the USA
Columbia, SC
12 February 2022

55641480R00102